THE OFFICIAL
DICTIONARY
OF
SARCASM

THE OFFICIAL
DICTIONARY
OF
SARCASM

A Lexicon for Those of Us
Who Are Better and Smarter
Than the Rest of You

JAMES NAPOLI
Executive Vice President
National Sarcasm Society

STERLING INNOVATION
An imprint of Sterling Publishing Co., Inc

New York / London
www.sterlingpublishing.com

ACKNOWLEDGMENTS

ACKNOWLEDGMENTS

This is the part of the book where the author thanks the eleven unpaid interns, who tirelessly proofread the manuscript; the dedicated agent, who slept with all the right people to make the deal happen; and the many long-suffering friends, who provided invaluable feedback throughout the process, as if they had any damn choice in the matter. There's also usually a nod to some kind of spousal unit, who remained patient and loving during the entire time the book was being written and with whom the author has probably begun divorce proceedings by the time the thing actually comes out. Except it went to press before things got really ugly, so the meaningless recognition paid to someone the author now wishes were dead perseveres for eternity.

But none of this is of any importance, because nobody ever reads this stupid page anyway.

SAR CASM 101

Though it hardly matters to a sarcastic person (who is most assuredly not in the business of making anyone feel better), those of you who appreciate sarcasm are a rare breed. Two major forces drive you: one is to provoke and the other is to seek the truth. Both of these life missions make people very uncomfortable. A provocateur is not always welcome at the finer dinner parties, and one who uses humor to get at what is really going on behind the words we use makes "the man" shake in his boots.

But you, who are now honorary members of the National Sarcasm Society simply by virtue of holding this book in your trembling hands, have never courted popularity. No, you are out there on the vanguard, waiting to eviscerate the innards of propriety and puncture the balloon of pretension.

Here, then, is your handbook. An *A-to-Z* guide to keep with you, should you ever need to set anyone straight on everything from beer to Bluetooth, from camping to karaoke, from Socrates to Spider-Man.

Use it as often as you wish, to challenge the tiny minds of the plebeian rabble with whom you come into contact on a daily basis. You have been waiting patiently for a dictionary like this to come along. And now it is here. Not that you give a crap.

WORDS YOU SHOULD KNOW

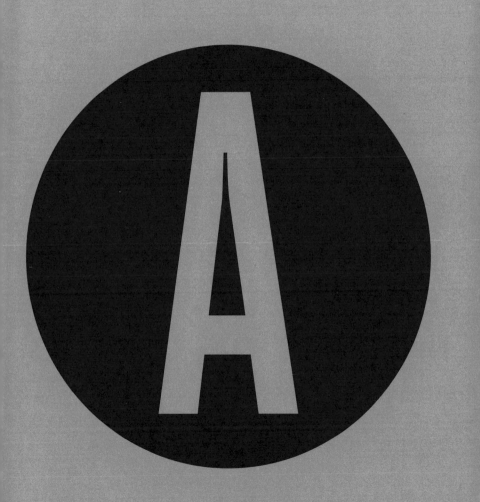

The Official Dictionary of Sarcasm

AARP: American Association of Retired Persons. An organization that sends out welcome letters to people over fifty to remind them that they will soon be dead.

ABBA: Swedish pop group whose catchy melodies are very useful in helping to illuminate which one of your friends is probably gay.

ABS: A part of the human body that can, apparently in only minutes a day as part of this exclusive TV offer, become rock hard.

ACADEMY AWARD: Recognition of achievement in the motion picture industry. Given annually to a group of people who are a hundred times prettier, richer, and more popular than you will ever be or have any hope of being.

ACCENT: A way of speaking that reflects the region of the world in which you grew up. Depending on where that it is and where you are when you use it, it could either get you beat up or laid.

ACCOUNTANT:
ONE OF A MYSTERIOUS RACE OF MOLE PEOPLE WHO RESURFACE ONCE A QUARTER AND CHARGE YOU TO USE QUICKEN.

ACHIEVEMENT: A great accomplishment, often accompanied by a sense of triumph. Or, as it is known to 98 percent of the population, getting out of bed in the morning.

ACID: Something you definitely have to be on to appreciate Carrot Top.

ACNE: Nature's way of telling you that you are not quite ready to have sex.

ACTIVIST: A person who cares about the fate of the world, until reaching approximately twenty-eight years of age.

ACTOR:

↓ ↓

→ A waiter.

ACTRESS:

↓ ↓

→ A waitress.

ACUPUNCTURIST: An alternative-medicine practitioner who gets to stab people and call it therapy.

AD HOC: A Latin phrase meaning "Hey, look at me, I know a Latin phrase."

ADORABLE: 1. The quality of being darling or cute. Usually confined to forwarded e-mails about kittens. 2. A word used by women in bars to refer to a man they want to say something nice about while making it painfully clear that they would never in a million years sleep with him.

ADULT: What you become when you finally give up drinking, sleeping around, and bouncing from job to job. Also known as kill-me-now syndrome.

ADVENTUROUS:

SOMETHING YOUR SPOUSE CLAIMED TO BE WHEN YOU FIRST STARTED DATING, BUT THE BEN WA BALLS ARE GATHERING DUST IN THE CLOSET AND IN ALL THIS TIME YOU'VE YET TO CRUISE THE BARS LOOKING TO SPICE THINGS UP.

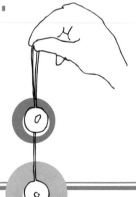

ADVERTISEMENT:

A MEDIUM THROUGH WHICH PEOPLE WHO TRULY CARE ABOUT YOUR WELFARE (AND NOT AT ALL ABOUT MONEY) PROVIDE YOU WITH HELPFUL, EXTREMELY SUBTLE REMINDERS THAT YOUR BAD BREATH, BODY ODOR, CELL PHONE PROVIDER, AND MAKE OF CAR ALL HAVE TO GO.

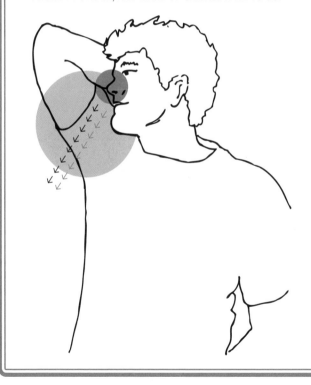

The Official Dictionary of Sarcasm

ADVICE: The only thing in the world more unwelcome than a baby in a movie theater.

AFFABLE: A workplace-based adjective used to describe the suck-up that always volunteers to replace the toner.

AFFLUENT: A word that allows you to describe a rich person without incorporating the usual tinge of jealousy and resentment.

AGGRESSIVE: A forceful, go-getter attitude that is greatly admired in business unless you are a woman.

AGLOW: The condition of being flush with radiant emotion, such as one in the bloom of love. Or, it might just be gas.

AGORAPHOBIA: A sudden attack of fear, anxiety, or panic—such as that brought about by the sudden realization that you forgot to clear your Internet history before leaving work today.

AIR:

THE GLORIOUS, GOD-GIVEN SUBSTANCE THAT PROVIDES US OUR VERY BREATH OF LIFE WHILE ALSO CONTAINING THE DISGUSTING, CONTAGIOUS PATHOGENS THAT WILL ONE DAY KILL US.

The Official Dictionary of Sarcasm

AIRBRUSH: An artist's tool invented by *Playboy* magazine to give your girlfriend an inferiority complex.

AIR-CONDITIONING: The glorious, man-made appliance that cools us in the heat of summer while blasting out recirculated air that contains the disgusting, contagious pathogens that will one day kill us.

AIRPLANE: A giant passenger vehicle whose entire operation will fail unless your seat backs and tray tables are in the upright and locked position.

AIRPORT: A mall placed near a large parking lot in which planes often land but rarely take off. To take your mind off the endless delays, these cavernous dungeons are populated by clueless security and ticket agents, zombie-like skycaps, and thousands of needlessly detained travelers enduring either the frustration of lost luggage or an impromptu body-cavity search. If Dante were alive today, airports would be listed as the fifth ring of Hell.

ALCOHOL: Awkwardness, foul breath, financial ruin, and the alienation of everybody who ever cared about you, all in handy liquid form, often with a twist-off cap.

ALIVE: The state of existing—of being cognizant of existence. Depending on just how much of your horrendous childhood you need to block out, this condition may not kick in until shortly after you graduate from high school.

ALLEN, WOODY:

SOME ELDERLY CREEP WHO MARRIED HIS BARELY COLLEGE-AGED ADOPTED STEPDAUGHTER. ALSO APPARENTLY MADE FILMS OR SOMETHING, ALTHOUGH ANY SUCH ACCOMPLISHMENT IS OFTEN USURPED BY THE ACT OF MARRYING HIS BARELY COLLEGE-AGED STEPDAUGHTER.

ALL RIGHT: What a man insists that he is whenever his significant other asks how he is feeling.

ALMOST: Just about, not quite, virtually, nearly, for all practical purposes . . . whatever. You freaking blew it, so just man up and admit it.

ALONE:

ISOLATED, FORSAKEN—FOR EXAMPLE, A GREEN PARTY POLITICIAN DURING A U.S. ELECTION CYCLE.

ALTERNATIVE: A type of music that pretentious, hipper-than-thou people like to say they listen to, completely oblivious to the fact that it has been labeled "alternative" by the same corporate machinery that makes all the other kinds of nonalternative music available for download on iTunes. Their pretentiousness is exacerbated by the fact that you can often catch these so-called cool people weeping while indulging in an MP3 of "Wind Beneath My Wings" when they think no one is looking.

AMATEUR: A beginner or aspirant in a given field; a non-professional as distinct from a practicing professional—except in the field of pornography, in which no such distinctions are necessary or even pertinent.

AMBIGUOUS:
EITHER THAT GAL IN HUMAN RESOURCES WHO WEARS BUTTON-DOWNS AND KHAKIS ALL THE TIME OR THAT GUY IN ACCOUNTS PAYABLE WHO ALWAYS HAS AN ASCOT COVERING HIS ADAM'S APPLE.

AMBITION: Nature's way of preparing us for heart medication.

AMERICA: An ongoing experiment in democracy controlled largely by insanely wealthy people. And that's just the way we like it, thank you very much.

AMISH:

A SECT OF SELF-SUSTAINING PEOPLE WHOSE WAY OF LIFE IS SO DIFFERENT FROM THE CURRENT IDEOLOGICAL MAINSTREAM THAT IT'S A WONDER NOBODY'S BOMBED THEM YET.

ANALOG: *Rare.* Recordings or television transmissions delivered nondigitally. While difficult to find, these strange devices do turn up on occasion, such as in the apartments of shut-ins or in the squirrel-infested cabins of half-mad, heavily armed conspiracy theorists.

ANARCHIST:
SOMEONE WHO ADVOCATES THE OVERTHROW OF THE EXISTING POWER STRUCTURE, OR JUST ANYONE WITH A GOATEE.

ANESTHETIC: Substance used by medical professionals who have no other way of shaving off someone's pubic hair without the person noticing.

ANGELS: Celestial beings that apparently have nothing better to do than hover around and make sure we get parking spaces and come to terms with getting cancer.

ANGER: Fury, outrage—such as that felt upon getting the news that you have cancer, until an angel drops by to calm you down and help you face your horrendous fate with dignity.

ANGST: A troubled state of mind that can make a person sullen and anxious. This can have a certain appeal when you are young, impressionable, and hopelessly naive enough to think you're going to be the one to change the angst-ridden person in question. This is a notion of which you are usually disabused after their third or fourth suicide attempt.

ANIMALS:

CREATURES THAT LEAVE US VERY FEW OPTIONS BESIDES HUNTING THEM, EATING THEM, KEEPING THEM AS PETS, OR LOCKING THEM IN A CAGE. THAT'S JUST HOW IT IS WHEN YOU HOLD DOMINION OVER ALL NATURE.

ANIMATION: A moving picture cartoon, usually featuring wisecracking anthropomorphized animals or sanitized reinterpretations of classic fairy tales. Animation can provide hours of downtime for adults who simply plunk their little ones in front of the television and let it hypnotize them into inactivity while the grown-ups kick back and try not to feel guilty about abdicating all responsibility as parents.

ANNIVERSARY: Try forgetting it, and you'll see what the hell it means.

ANT: An insect of the family Formicidae, colonies of which have been around for 130 million years and have succeeded in occupying almost every landmass on earth. Kind of puts your bachelor's in business administration in perspective, doesn't it?

ANTSY: What irritating, twitchy people were before they had the luxury of saying they had something called restless leg syndrome.

APARTMENT: A place to throw your money away on rent before you throw your money away on a mortgage.

APATHY: A state of uninterest bordering on lethargy. Ask any retail clerk for assistance to experience this phenomenon first hand.

APPLAUSE: An obligatory expression of approval for someone's half-assed form of creative expression that arises more from relief that the experience is finally over than from a genuine feeling of having been entertained.

The Official Dictionary of Sarcasm

APPLIANCE:
SOMETHING A MAN GIVES
HIS WIFE FOR HER BIRTHDAY
TO NONE TOO SUBTLY
INDICATE THAT THE SEXUAL
SPARK BETWEEN THEM IS
HORRIBLY, IRRETRIEVABLY
GONE.

APPRECIATE: A word commonly used by superiors to indicate that they want you to do a task patently outside of your job description and that doing it will result in their undying gratitude and heartfelt admiration but absolutely no pay. *"I would appreciate it if you would go over to the filing cabinets and alphabetize the last sixteen years of active sales leads before Tuesday."*

ARCHIMEDES: Greek scientist, born 287 BC. One of the main guys responsible for giving the world math. Thanks a lot, you bastard.

ARCHITECT: A bold, forward-thinking leader who guides teams of designers in the creation of the world's dwellings and great buildings of commerce and industry. The typical architect starts out with grand, sweeping visions of making an impact similar to that of Frank Lloyd Wright, only to end up being in charge of revamping the neighborhood Chuck E. Cheese's.

ARISTOTLE: Greek philosopher, born 384 BC. Though his name is world famous, he remains one of those guys you hope nobody ever asks you a question about.

ART: The deliberate arrangement of elements in any given medium in such a way as to appeal to the aesthetic sense. If the last few centuries are any indication, most works of art could easily have been painted by the five-year-old child of whoever is viewing the work at the time.

ARTISTIC: Having skills or ability in a creative field. It is surprisingly easy to identify artistic talent during youth, as the budding artists are usually the ones getting the crap kicked out of them at recess.

ASSEMBLY LINE: A process perfected in the early twentieth century that allowed for mass production and ushered in the modern consumer age while simultaneously taking all the individuality out of labor and turning workers into brain-dead zombies. Not to mention brain-dead zombies with carpal tunnel syndrome.

ATHEIST: A person who privately prays that they don't turn out to be wrong.

ATTILA THE HUN: Leader of a band of Central Asian nomads from 434 to 453; his invading armies cut a swath through many regions of Europe, little realizing that they would all be forgotten while their lousy boss got all the credit and became synonymous with merciless savagery. Typical.

ATTRACTION: The most mysterious of all laws of human interaction, especially when it concerns someone who dumped your ass and is now with someone thirty pounds heavier than you.

AUNT:
THE SISTER OF ONE'S FATHER OR MOTHER. A WOMAN CONGENITALLY OBLIGATED TO SPIT INTO HER HANDKERCHIEF AND THEN USE THE DISGUSTING SNOT RAG TO WIPE SOMETHING OFF YOUR FACE. MORE FRIGHTENING VARIETIES OF AUNTS ALSO WEAR HATS WITH PLASTIC FRUIT ON THEM.

AUTOMOBILE: An individual land transport vehicle used mainly to provoke the extension of the human middle finger.

AWESOME: A word most properly used to denote something truly breathtaking, unbelievably magnificent, or strikingly wonderful; it is now used to describe everything from a half-decent meal to a show of support for someone who just landed an entry-level job at Staples.

BABY: Though nothing more than an extremely tiny human highly adept at eating and defecating, somehow these howling, underdeveloped, and often quite ugly creatures manage to command all the damn attention in the room.

BABY BUMP: A term frequently used by the media to describe the gently protruding abdomen of a female celebrity. The implication is, of course, that it is only a bump and that the previously anorexic, bulimic celebrity, who was also kept concentration-camp thin by all manner of prescription appetite suppressants, should not be considered fat just yet.

BABYSITTER:

A HIGH SCHOOL GIRL WHO HAS THE MYSTERIOUS ABILITY TO MAKE YOUR CHILD—WHO, WHENEVER YOU ARE AROUND, NEVER GIVES YOU A MOMENT'S PEACE—SOMEHOW SLEEP SOUNDLY FOR THE ENTIRE TIME YOU ARE OUT AT THE MOVIES, THEREFORE GETTING PAID ANYWHERE FROM TWENTY TO FIFTY BUCKS TO ESSENTIALLY SIT IN YOUR HOUSE AND WATCH TELEVISION UNTIL YOU COME HOME.

The Official Dictionary of Sarcasm

BABY STROLLER: Difficult to distinguish from a small armored vehicle, the modern stroller is apparently designed to make sure your child can survive a sudden and unexpected encounter with a herd of charging wildebeests. Of course, should such a thing occur, by the time you unclasp the nine different clips holding your little one in the stroller seat, disengage the stroller canopy, knock back the stroller umbrella attachment, and unzip the stroller netting, you yourself will be horribly maimed by the unfortunate wildebeest onslaught. But, in your own way, you will have protected your child, which, ironically, was the reason you bought the stroller in the first place.

BAGGAGE: After around three months of passionate sex and feeling giddy with new love, a couple begins to realize they are now in an honest-to-God relationship. At this stage, baggage is something you slowly start to realize your new boyfriend/girlfriend has got up the wazoo.

BAGGAGE CAROUSEL: A whirring contraption on which you keep seeing the same suitcase, which looks like yours but is actually someone else's, go by thirty times and yet every single time it comes around again, you still think it's yours for just a second or two. This is a phenomenon brought about by the insane hope that the airline has not lost your luggage.

BAGGAGE HANDLER: A person paid not to care if he or she breaks all your stuff.

BALLS: Something you have to, however begrudgingly, give telemarketers credit for.

BAND: A group formed half-heartedly in high school in the hope of meeting girls. Starting out with mastering the opening guitar riff from "Smoke on the Water" and progressing to two-hour rehearsals in the drummer's parents' garage, the group of acne-ridden misfits eventually specializes in anemic covers of Led Zeppelin, Nirvana, and Aerosmith. Much discussion goes into their name, with suggestions ranging from "Bilbo's Hat" to "Frothing Mongoose." At last, the band plays one high school dance where their amps blow twenty minutes into the set. They summarily break up, although one of them keeps threatening to get everybody back together again to watch their ill-fated debut, documented on VHS that night by some geek from the AV Club.

BANK: A place to enjoy waiting in line when you can't make it to the post office.

BANKRUPT: A state of financial destitution. Also a morally bankrupt person, which, ironically, usually describes someone who never actually experiences being literally bankrupt, because being a greedy, egotistical a-hole usually keeps you well out of the red.

BAR: A place where lonely, desperate people go to get hammered enough to find other lonely, desperate people suddenly irresistible.

BARISTA: A PERSON HIGHLY SKILLED IN WRITING YOUR FIRST NAME IN SHARPIE ON THE SIDE OF A HEAT-TREATED PAPER CUP.

BARTENDER: A psychotherapist who keeps a damp rag slung over a shoulder.

BASEBALL: A spectator sport known as "the great American pastime" largely because so much time passes while waiting for each game to end. There are many traditions associated with a day at the ballpark, including the consumption of sodium-rich foods and a beer-like substance that may actually be reconstituted urine. There is also the charming tradition of the park organist, whose many prompts get the crowd to cheer "Charge!" optimistically, even when their team is behind by sixteen runs in the top of the ninth inning. Baseball fans are known for their love of statistics, including batting averages, RBIs, and ERAs. Another interesting statistic is that one could combine the yearly income of every working-stiff fan seated in the left-field bleacher section and it still would not equal the weekly salary of the average bench warmer.

BASKETBALL: A fast-paced and energetic team sport in which two opposing teams attempt to score the most points by propelling a large orange ball through a hoop roughly ten feet off the ground. The game is notable mostly for the fact that it is played in stadiums that used to have some individuality but are now named after a wide variety of telephone companies and office supply retailers.

BATHROOM: A room in the home often festooned with brightly colored tiles and seashell-shaped dishes filled with unusually scented handmade soaps and potpourri, all to try and offset the fact that most of what goes on there involves number one, number two, and questionable hairs stuck in the shower drain.

BATMAN:
A COMIC BOOK CRIME FIGHTER WHOSE ON-SCREEN PERSONA WENT FROM CAMPY AND IRREVERENT IN THE 1960S TO BROODING AND DAMN NEAR SUICIDAL IN THE TWENTY-FIRST CENTURY. OF COURSE, THIS MAY OR MAY NOT SAY ANYTHING ABOUT WHERE WE ARE HEADED AS A SPECIES.

BEACH: A place where the majestic ocean and its miles of luxurious sand are transformed into a petri dish of potential staph infections by an unruly mob of overstressed people trying to get their folding chairs and beach umbrellas to stay put, many of whom did not get the memo about how having a prodigious pot belly and wearing a Speedo simply do not mix.

BEATLES, THE:
OBSCURE LIVERPOOL ROCK AND ROLL BAND OF VERY LITTLE NOTE OR INFLUENCE.

BEAUTIFUL: Something that is pleasing to the eye—such as the sight of the Porsche that has been weaving in and out of lanes for the past ten minutes actually getting pulled over. Yes! Beautiful!

BEAUTY: Allure or attractiveness—the male ideal often represented by Adonis, the eternally youthful god of ancient Greece; the female ideal often represented by Venus, the Roman goddess of love and fertility. Of course, most of us fall way short of these ideals and can be better described as being somewhere between Angelina Jolie and the Elephant Man.

BECAUSE: A word that passes for an explanation as to why children must do as you say.

BED: An item of furniture that was originally designed for the simple, restful act of slumber, and one that most young couples actually put to that purpose shortly after marriage.

BEER: A beverage about which some rather laughable people believe it is possible to be a "connoisseur," despite the fact that the main difference between most beers is which one tastes the least like liquid ass.

BEGGAR: Someone reduced to soliciting strangers for charity. Or, as it is known in some circles, Girl Scouts.

BELIEF: An absolute certainty that something is true. Can range from one's opinion as to whether there is a God to the firm conviction that space aliens are sending coded messages through your fillings.

BELT: A band of material used to encircle and support a round object. Most modern belts include a helpful series of holes punched out in them, so that as the farthermost holes are utilized over time, one may track one's own repulsive slide into utter fatness. Annually, following the American celebration of Thanksgiving, bulging midriffs are given a pass and men are allowed to undo their belts and let their turkey-bloated stomachs spill from their unbuttoned trousers with pride as they watch more active and physically fit members of society play football on television.

BEST: A word denoting something matchless, choice, without peer; extremely useful when lying. *"Gosh, future mother-in-law, that was the best meal I've ever eaten." "Gosh, new boyfriend, that was the best sex I ever had."*

BETTER: Somewhere between good and best. Usually code-speak for "you suck a little less than you sucked before, but you have a long way to go before you are entirely without suckiness."

BIASED: What pissed-off liberals call people they suspect might have a point.

BICYCLE:

A PEDAL-DRIVEN, HUMAN-POWERED CONVEYANCE USED BY PEOPLE WHO THINK THEY'RE MAKING SOME KIND OF BIG STATEMENT ABOUT THE ENVIRONMENT JUST BY RIDING ONE. SURE, THEY'RE ALL IN BETTER SHAPE THAN YOU COULD EVER HOPE TO BE, AND, OK, SO SOMETIMES THEY RIDE 10K MARATHONS TO RAISE MONEY FOR LEUKEMIA RESEARCH AND EVERYTHING, BUT WHAT THEY DON'T KNOW IS THAT THEY LOOK GEEKY IN THOSE HELMETS. SO THERE.

BIG BEN:

A BIG CLOCK. ONLY THE BRITISH WOULD THINK THAT THAT WAS ANYTHING.

BIRTHDAY: One's date of birth. The only day of the year when you can receive a card from someone professing to be your friend that includes a so-called humorous reference to how freaking old you are and how you probably are all dried up or can't get it up anymore. A topic of conversation that might otherwise get this so-called friend punched in the jaw, this sentiment is somehow OK to convey when it is delivered in a card featuring a black-and-white line drawing of a decrepit octogenarian nodding off in a nursing home rocking chair. And you're supposed to smile and take it. Happy birthday, indeed.

BISEXUAL: Something that a guy wouldn't half mind his girlfriend being, although if his girlfriend wanted it the other way around, it would probably make him throw up.

BIT RATE: The number of bits of information that are processed digitally per unit of time. Whatever. I mean, honestly, isn't this the stuff we pay IT to know?

BLACKBEARD: Real name: Edward Teach. Notorious eighteenth-century pirate who had the whole weird androgynous thing down way before Johnny Depp.

BLACKBERRY: A device created to satisfy man's apparently inbred nature to check something every fifteen damn seconds.

The Official Dictionary of Sarcasm

BLACKBOARD: An ancient item uncovered in recent archeological expeditions. Apparently a slate device on which one could scrawl pertinent information with chalk to relay said information to gatherings of young people who would then use something called *pens* to transfer the information to something called *paper*. Strange, but true.

BLACKSMITH: A person who forges iron, his beautifully muscled arms glistening with sweat as he works in perfect concert with an anvil and hammer, shaping and molding the once-unyielding metal with the heat of a fiery furnace, the orange flames licking at his rippling, moist skin. And still these guys can't get their own calendar.

BLENDER: A home appliance used to make tasty beverage concoctions. Employed chiefly by people who think drinking a margarita makes them less of a boozer than the homeless rotgut-swigging inebriates they will one day become.

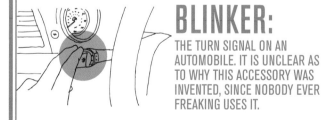

BLINKER:
THE TURN SIGNAL ON AN AUTOMOBILE. IT IS UNCLEAR AS TO WHY THIS ACCESSORY WAS INVENTED, SINCE NOBODY EVER FREAKING USES IT.

BLISS: A state of being in which everything suddenly makes sense and one is consumed by a feeling of interconnectedness with the universe. Often occurs for approximately 1.5 seconds after sex, just before you suddenly remember that you left the DVD on pause.

BLOW: A word with many meanings, none of which are as dirty as what you are thinking right now.

BLOG:

ANY OF VARIOUS INTERNET DESTINATIONS MAINTAINED BY TRAGICALLY DELUDED PEOPLE WHO ACTUALLY THINK YOU ARE INTERESTED IN THEIR ALL-TIME FAVORITE COREY HAIM MOVIES, THEIR TYPO-INFESTED RANTS ABOUT THE DATING SCENE, OR THEIR MINUTE-BY-MINUTE UPDATES CHRONICLING THE GROWTH OF THEIR MEWLING, VOMIT-STAINED INFANT CAPTURED IN QUICKTIME VIDEO.

BLOOD: A plasma-based fluid running through your veins that unfortunately links you to some of the biggest jerks on the planet. And even now, long after you have left home, this same fluid requires you to grit your teeth and get together with them at least once a year, if only to reaffirm your belief that you couldn't possibly be related to these losers.

BLUETOOTH: A wireless device placed directly in the ear, allowing well-dressed businessmen to be indistinguishable from the ragged skid row lunatic who is also walking around having a loud, obnoxious conversation with someone who isn't there.

BOAT: A vessel meant for traveling on water, which is commonly taken to sea a grand total of one time before the realization hits that it is an unwieldy, high-maintenance money-suck that was really only purchased to prove something to all those bastards in high school who said you would never make it.

BODY: Something women can never let go if they want to keep their man. Something men can feel free to let go as long as they make enough money.

BODY SHOP: A place containing people who didn't bother to waste money on college and are now earning sixteen times more than saps like you who did.

BOOK:

AN OBJECT THAT CONFERS UPON ITS OWNER A CERTAIN AIR OF ATTRACTIVENESS AND UNBRIDLED SEXUAL DYNAMISM. (THIS ENTRY CONTRACTUALLY REQUIRED BY AUTHOR.)

BOOKMARK: Either a strip of material placed between the pages of a book to mark a place, or an Internet identifier to enable a quick and easy return to a Web site. Probably the latter unless you're, like, a hundred or something.

BORDER: A line between geographical regions. Often zealously guarded, to prevent the people who want to come over and do the jobs no one else wants to do from getting in.

BORING: Something you instinctively know the ballet, opera, and performance art are, but never mention because somewhere inside you think the person who dragged you out to this crap may actually understand it.

BOSS: An underqualified moron who you cannot believe was hired by those other morons in HR and whose job you are certain you could do about a million times better.

BOTTLED WATER:

TAP WATER MADE MORE PALATABLE BY A LABEL WITH A MOUNTAIN ON IT.

BOUNCE HOUSE: An inflatable recreational device that gives parents of young children the illusion of a few moments of peace. It achieves this by allowing them to shunt their progeny into a giant vinyl room and forget about them for a good portion of the party. Ironically, the screams of delight, combined with the deafening clamor of the generator, are actually more annoying than anything they have to put up with at home.

BOWLING: An indoor sport played by rolling a ball toward a set of pins in hopes of knocking them down, all while drinking beer and sitting down for long intervals waiting for your turn to come up again. Perhaps the most liberal definition of *exercise* known to man.

BOX: A cardboard container used for storage and shipping. Once plentiful and readily available by simply getting off one's ass and going to the trouble of visiting one's local supermarket to request any unused boxes they may have. Now, however, mankind is reduced to visiting a *box store* in which cheap cardboard cartons can be purchased for as much as twenty-five dollars simply because they have a company logo printed on them. Inexplicably, customers have chosen this arrangement over the previously free exchange of receptacles for no discernable reason other than that they are douches.

BOXING: One day, somebody mentioned that it might be interesting to let two men pummel each other about the face and body, preferably to the point of inflicting cerebral hemorrhage, while a bunch of people watched. And then somebody else said that sounded like a pretty good idea. Sometimes, life is pretty uncomplicated.

BRAIN: An organ that is the center for the management of all bodily activities by receiving and sending information to muscles and organs, and the holder of human consciousness, memory, and emotion. That is, until something in a short skirt walks into the room, at which point all of these functions are immediately taken over by the penis.

BRANDO, MARLON: Iconic American method actor whose most convincing performance was in the role of a guy becoming a total weirdo, gaining a lot of weight, and then dying.

BREAK ROOM: A space in the workplace set aside for employees to relax when they are not on duty. In reality, it remains unoccupied except by antisocial losers who bring their own lunch and don't seem to mind that they are squandering what could be a very rejuvenating hour away from this gaping maw of hell known as their job.

BREASTS: Milk-producing glandular organs located between the neck and torso of a woman. When described in this way, one can observe how any component of sexual attraction is removed from the equation, so a rational discussion of these miracles of nature can ensue. This should last about eight seconds, at which point somebody is going to break down and call them "funbags."

BRIDGE: A structure invented by our founding fathers, who long ago surveyed the land and asked themselves the question, How best can we hose our citizenry out of a three dollar toll?

BROMANCE: Intense, loving friendship between two men. All the convenience of a same-sex relationship without having to wait for your state to lift the gay marriage ban.

BROTHER: 1. One's male sibling. You know, the one you will never live up to no matter how hard you try. 2. Something white people call black people in the vain and self-serving hope of implying that they are somehow "down with the struggle."

BUCKINGHAM PALACE: A centuries-old estate in which a bunch of obscenely rich, inbred, nonelected twats hang out in powdered wigs while waiting for their next chance to wave from the back of a horse-drawn carriage.

BUDDHA:

THE ONLY DISGUSTING FOUR-HUNDRED-POUND MAN PEOPLE ACTUALLY CHOOSE TO EMULATE, BUDDHA IS THE FIRST MORBIDLY OBESE GUY WITH FOOD ISSUES TO DEVELOP AN INSANELY LOYAL FOLLOWING.

BUDGET: The allocation of funds over a set period of time for a particular series of expenditures. Usually shot to hell by the sudden need for braces, a new timing belt, or liposuction.

BUMPER STICKER: A statement on a piece of heavy paper backed with gummed adhesive and placed on the rear bumper of one's car. Developed exclusively for self-absorbed yuppie parents whose only acknowledgement of the existence of the trophy children they pawn off to the care of a nanny comes from letting the car behind them know that one of the little twerps was recently named Student of the Month.

BURNOUT: A state of complete exhaustion brought on by being engaged in something unpleasant for far too long a time. Usually occurring in a workplace environment, but also applicable to a relationship that has run its course. I mean, this thing is dead and we both know it. Can't we just stop pretending and let it rot? Let its decomposing carcass provide the final testament to the pointlessness of continuing on with such a hideous charade? Sorry, L. W., I knew you would be reading this, and I just couldn't think of any other way to tell you.

BURRITO:
A DELICIOUS WAY TO ALIENATE THE GUESTS AT THE PARTY YOU WILL SOON BE ATTENDING.

BUS: A response to your city planner's challenge of combining a hospital for the criminally insane with a trash receptacle and a slum and putting the whole experience on wheels for your convenience.

BUSINESS: An occupation or trade at which a person makes one's living. Often, one's business can be a rewarding and meaningful way to provide a service to the community while gaining individual job satisfaction.

BUSINESS, BIG: An organization dedicated to grinding dreams into the dirt.

BUT: A conjunction used to indicate a contrary viewpoint or exception. *"I wanted to make something of my life, but since I am stoned all the time, I could never get my act together." "I'm sorry I firebombed your office, but you promised you'd get back to me within a week after the interview."*

BUTT: By simply adding one *t* to the end of the previous word, you get to introduce the subject of the human ass. English is a remarkable language.

BUZZKILL: Someone who brings up the subject of world hunger during a lap dance.

CABLE:

AN INCREDIBLE SCAM PERPETRATED ON THE TELEVISION VIEWING PUBLIC, IN WHICH THEY ARE OFTEN CHARGED MORE THAN ONE HUNDRED DOLLARS PER MONTH FOR THE PRIVILEGE OF TAKING IN THE OCCASIONAL EXCLUSIVE SPORTING EVENT, A TWENTY-FOUR-HOUR WEATHER CHANNEL, AND THE HERETOFORE UNHEARD OF OPPORTUNITY TO WATCH *SPIES LIKE US* FOURTEEN TIMES IN ONE WEEK.

CADDY: 1. An adolescent nonbeing that is trained to hump bags for obnoxious, stuck-up CEOs who realize that it is their unspoken right to treat him like garbage. 2. An automobile whose status conveyed class on mobsters and pimps in the years 1955 through 1985.

CAESAR, JULIUS: Dictator of ancient Rome. His nearly fifteen years of conquest, which resulted in the formation of the entire Roman Empire; now reduced to a salad.

CAFFEINE: Everything that is right and good with the world contained in one alkaloid compound. Truly, this substance is proof of the existence of God.

CALENDAR: An object that exists in order that the phenomenal backlog of cute puppy photos may be put to some use each and every year until the end of time.

CALM: What you are usually urged to remain around the time the third engine on the aircraft has failed.

CAMP: A traditional summer rite of passage for the preadolescent, camp involves a series of outdoor activities designed to foster even more unhealthy competition than its participants undergo at school and to subject a terrified group of unwilling misfit children to

The Official Dictionary of Sarcasm

an endless barrage of humiliation and physical torture at the hands of bullies and clueless counselors alike. Designed to toughen and prepare the young person for the vicissitudes life will bring, it more often than not creates a new generation ready to contribute to society by becoming proud serial killers of the future.

CAMPING: An absolute must for anyone who has not yet experienced the thrill of lying in the pitch black middle of nowhere wondering what that scratching noise is outside the tent that is rapidly lowering itself onto you; surviving on unsalted almonds and dehydrated macaroni and cheese barely heated over a cook stove, most of which sticks to the bottom of the thinnest excuse for a saucepan you have ever seen; and being granted the honor of having to dig the very hole in which you are going to take a crap. Three days of this, and you will sell your body on the street corner for one hour in a hotel.

CANADA: Free health care. Low crime. Birthplace of William Shatner. Two out of three ain't bad.

CANDLE: As something to give as a present when you are completely incapable of coming up with anything original, this is right up there with a gift certificate.

CAPONE, AL:

NOTORIOUS CHICAGO MOBSTER WHOSE SMUGGLING AND BOOTLEGGING OPERATIONS DOMINATED THE 1920S CRIME SCENE. THOUGH HE WAS COMMONLY KNOWN AS SCARFACE, THERE IS NO RECORD OF HIM EVER SAYING, "SAY HELLO TO MY LITTLE FRIEND."

CAPPUCCINO: Coffee for those who need to hear a large, ear-splitting, Darth Vader–like sucking sound moments before their beverage is served.

CAR ALARM: An antitheft device that only goes off when no one is trying to steal your car.

CARE: What you have, or will one day, put your parents in. And where, one day, your offspring will put you. As with most words used by the medical profession, it is designed to provide comfort to the lousy, no-good kids who repay a lifetime of love and support from mom and dad by sticking them into some *Cuckoo's Nest*–like hellhole to live out the rest of their days.

CAREFREE: An untroubled and cheerful demeanor. Usually exhibited by empty-headed jackasses who don't know how bad things really are.

CAREFUL: Something men promise to be roughly nine months before the baby is born.

CARNIVORE: One who gets pleasure out of eating the flesh of vegetarians.

CASHIER: An individual who at one time was required to think and calculate basic math equations in his or her head, but whose modern-day duties consist of learning how to wave something over a scanner until it beeps and making as little eye contact with you as possible while funneling your two bags' worth of purchases into eight individual nonrecyclable plastic sacks.

CASTRO, FIDEL:

REVOLUTIONARY LEADER AND SOCIALIST PRESIDENT OF CUBA FROM 1976 TO 2008. ONLY MAN IN HISTORY TO HAVE A TOTAL OF 78,652 SECRET DOCUMENTS PERTAINING TO THE OVERTHROW OF THE U.S. GOVERNMENT CONCEALED IN HIS BEARD.

CASUAL FRIDAY: A weekly reprieve of the workplace dress code designed to (a) give employees the illusion that they have a modicum of control over the corporate decision-making process even though they will never be anything more than highly dispensable, undervalued cogs in a system that is intent on grinding them into a pulpy mass and (b) suggest to these same luckless plebeians that their bosses are even remotely capable of doing anything fun or spontaneous, when in reality they have some of the largest sticks known to man shoved permanently up their backsides.

CAT: A creature for which you continue to provide food and shelter despite the fact that it hates you and wishes you were dead.

CATATONIC: A state of extreme stupor. Most commonly seen in college freshmen taking classes with titles like "Introduction to Semiotics," the condition is also prevalent among local news anchorpersons in the smaller markets.

CATFIGHT: The closest most men will ever get to the witnessing of lesbian activity; as such, a highly prized event in their sad little lives.

CATHETER: If a hollow tube inserted into one or more of your body cavities to enable the passage of fluid through the system isn't God's way of telling you you're just about done, I don't know what is.

CATTY: Snide or spiteful. Usually in the context of a remark about someone's appearance. Women use catty remarks much more commonly, since the level of personal grooming among their peers is a matter of some concern to them. Men, however, have no use for the catty remark, as most of the guys they know are also smelly, unfashionable, and pot-bellied palookas who take pride in hanging on to a pair of underwear so threadbare and thin that it resembles rice paper.

CAULK: A sealant used in home repair. Commonly kept around the house by men who need to occasionally give the appearance of contributing to the upkeep of the home with some vaguely manly activity. Interestingly, the word is a sound-alike for the part of a man's body that creates the aforementioned need.

CC: A notation that appears at the bottom of interoffice memos to indicate the other three suckers who will be blamed when everything hits the fan.

CD: Compact disc. A now ancient delivery system for recorded music that for some inexplicable reason fell out of favor, since it only had about a 900 percent mark up and forced you to pay twenty bucks for an album with one good song on it, while the same song could now be downloaded off the Internet, often at no cost. As mentioned, it is difficult to see how this remarkable technology failed to endure.

CELERY: Despite a few pitiful attempts to make this flavorless plant edible by stuffing its crevice with peanut butter or sour cream and garlic dip, celery remains the most useless of God's creations and should be eliminated from the face of the earth.

CELL PHONE: A communication device developed by a team of scientists who were determined to make sure no one would ever be left the hell alone again.

CEMETERY: A place with a lot of people, none of whom are capable of cutting you off in traffic, playing their TV loud while you're trying to sleep, or letting their dog crap on your lawn. There is some comfort to be taken in that.

CEO:
A PERSON WHO WEARS A TIE WITH HIS ORANGE JUMPSUIT.

CERAMICS: That one adult education class your girlfriend forced you to attend with her, which resulted in your apartment being briefly overrun by all manner of misshapen earthenware.

CGI: Computer-generated imagery. A technique used by movies to remind us that we are watching something with no discernible story or character development.

CHANGE: Something homeless people can no longer ask you to spare, since the last time you used anything but plastic to buy even a pack of gum dates back to the previous millennium.

CHAOS: A state of extreme disorder. Captured perfectly in nature by the contents of a woman's handbag.

CHAPLIN, CHARLIE: Legendary silent-film-era comedian, known for his loveable tramp persona and for giving boring people with no imagination an idea for a Halloween costume.

CHARISMA: Extraordinary personal magnetism. Commonly possessed by politicians and movie stars or anyone else whose sick need for public approbation has manifested itself in a borderline personality disorder that ends up destroying the lives of all it touches. And, of course, instilling embittered jealousy in all those who do not possess it, such as the authors of sarcasm dictionaries.

CHARITY: Something you could swear your significant other continues to sleep with you out of.

CHASTE: Morally pure; decent. A quality known in the dating scene as a waste of your time and effort.

CHAUFFEUR: A man whose job it is to continue looking straight ahead while people have sex in his back seat.

CHEAP: Easily obtainable at low cost. Note that this greatly increases the risk of crabs.

CHEAT: To defraud or swindle; also to be unfaithful in a relationship. The former could land you in jail; the latter will land you in the doghouse. It is up to you decide which would be the more guilt-ridden, soul-destroying experience.

CHECK: What always ends up getting divided equally by all your so-called friends at the restaurant, even though the crafty bastards had full entrees and six beers each and all you ordered was a side salad and a Sprite.

CHEESE: Something you add to your hamburger to increase your odds of getting arteriosclerosis.

CHEMICALS: Substances arrived at through chemistry—some form of which that compulsive pencil-tapper in the cubicle next to you is clearly on.

CHEWING TOBACCO:

SMOKELESS TOBACCO. NAMED AS SUCH BECAUSE IT IS PINCHED BETWEEN THE CHEEK AND GUM AND THEREFORE PRODUCES NOT SMOKE, BUT A DROOLING, BROWN, MUCOUS-LIKE STRING OF SPITTLE THAT IS NOT ONLY A DELIGHT TO SEE IN ACTION, BUT EVEN MORE FUN TO PAINSTAKINGLY SCRAPE FROM THE FLOORS OF DUGOUTS AFTER NINE INNINGS OF BASEBALL.

CHICKEN: Domestic fowl; should not be confused with the frightening, alien subspecies that you will get if you order chicken at any restaurant with a drive-through.

CHIEF: A word used by men to address other men whom they secretly disdain. It is a word that, on the surface, appears to indicate a level of respect and camaraderie, but is really all most he-men can muster when meeting that one friend of a friend who actually makes a living teaching Elizabethan poetry.

CHILDISH: A word that has a negative connotation to stuck-up people who don't think farts or laughing milk through your nose is funny.

CHILDREN: Miniature versions of yourself who are hell-bent on leaving you half-mad and penniless.

CHIVALRY: Considerate behavior that a man completely abandons right after as many dates as it takes to get a woman into bed.

CHOCOLATE: Substance used as a peace offering as many times as needed to make up for the chivalry that ended right after you got her into bed.

CHOKE:

AN ACTION THAT ONLY THE THOUGHT OF ENDLESSLY PROTRACTED LEGAL PROCEEDINGS KEEPS YOU FROM CARRYING OUT ON YOUR BOSS.

The Official Dictionary of Sarcasm

CHOKED UP: To be stricken with an onrush of tearful emotion that is just barely kept at bay. A condition used to great effect by lying scumbags who want people to think they are actually repentant when being interviewed by *60 Minutes*.

CHRISTMAS: The holiday on December 25 commemorating the birth of a man who begged us to eschew personal possessions. Celebrated annually by many people trampling each other half to death in hopes of getting the last Tickle Me Elmo.

CHURCH: A place where children under the age of twelve are contractually obligated to laugh inappropriately just because they are not supposed to.

CHURCHILL, SIR WINSTON: British prime minister who served his first term during World War II. Known for his many forthright quotations, including, "We shall fight them on the beaches, we shall fight on the landing grounds, we shall fight in the fields and in the streets . . . Oh, and when I say *we*, I mean a bunch of people other than me."

CIGAR: A large, smoking, tube-shaped object, that is often rolled seductively between the fingers while being inserted into one's mouth. Draw your own conclusions.

CIGARETTE: Tobacco rolled in paper for smoking. Often derided for its cancer-causing properties by people who are jealous of how cool it makes you look.

CITY: A place that offers the allure of all the same chain stores they have in the suburbs, along with crime, filth, questionable transactions in disease-infested back alleys, and a chance to see a road company production of *The Producers*.

CITY OFFICIAL: Someone who routinely puts the needs of his or her constituency after his or her own self-serving desires. No, that was not a typo.

CLASS: 1. The quality of possessing higher standards or an elegance of taste. Many people from New Jersey confuse this condition with showing the neighbors how much faux-marble Greek and Roman statuary they can display on one lawn. 2. Something any intelligent college student should know better than to schedule for 9 a.m., when he or she will still be hungover.

CLASSIFIEDS: The part of the newspaper you persist in scanning for help-wanted ads, even though something tells you the job of your dreams might be difficult to find in the same section in which people are selling their used backhoe or a rabid pit bull or hoping to get a reply to their posting in "Men Seeking Hermaphrodites."

The Official Dictionary of Sarcasm

CLAUSTROPHOBIA: A fear of enclosed places. Frequently experienced by former college students who recall the trauma of paying three grand a month for a roach-infested apartment the size of a soap dish just so they could tell their friends they were living the dream in Manhattan.

CLEANING:
SOMETHING MANY POOR IMMIGRANTS HAVE TO DO TWICE: ONCE FOR THEMSELVES AND ONCE FOR THE PRICKLY RICH LADY WITH THE BRATTY KIDS WHO PAYS THEM NEXT TO NOTHING UNDER THE TABLE AND WOULD BE THE FIRST TO DENY EVER KNOWING THEM IF HOMELAND SECURITY CAME A-KNOCKIN'.

CLEOPATRA: Legendary hottie and Egyptian pharaoh from 51–30 BC. Known for her love affairs with Julius Caesar and Mark Antony and for committing suicide with a poison asp. In twenty-one years of rule, you would think she might have been remembered for a few other accomplishments, but apparently *schtupping* two famous guys on a regular basis and offing herself with a snake was all they covered on *Access: Egypt*.

CLOSET:
SOMETHING THAT ONE FLAMBOYANT COUSIN OF YOURS STILL REFUSES TO COME OUT OF.

CLOWN: An entertainer in a circus, known for slapstick antics and buffoonery. Ironically, these make-up enhanced, Rudolph-nosed jesters are designed to amuse and delight young children, when in reality they are nothing to a child if not a source of eerie, inexplicable terror. This fear causes deep emotional scarring that continues into adulthood, causing perfectly rational grown-ups to shudder involuntarily whenever they see someone with a painted-on smile and balloon pants.

COACH: 1. Usually a fairly unremarkable gym teacher or a nondescript neighborhood parent who donates time to fostering a cooperative spirit among young people. Yet somehow such stories have inspired Hollywood to depict coaches as washed-up boozers who have made a mess of their lives and alienated all those who love them, and whose only chance at redemption lies in reluctantly leading a ragtag team of misfits to victory against all odds, thereby discovering their own long-untapped potential.

COCA-COLA: A soft drink whose makers are apparently morally obligated to dream up a new version of the same sugar, water, and caffeine they have always sold every eight weeks until the end of time.

COCKROACH:

ANY OF A TYPE OF FLAT-BODIED INSECTS THAT ARE INCLUDED AS PART OF YOUR RENTAL AGREEMENT.

COCKTAIL: A word that contains a certain appeal in and of itself (as in the designation of a mixed alcoholic beverage), as well as inviting fairly positive connotations when preceded by the word *shrimp*. Yet, amazingly, the term can easily be rendered utterly repugnant by simply putting the word *fruit* in front of it.

COFFEE: A laxative that you can buy in the same places that sell croissants.

COLISEUM, THE: A hugely significant feat of Roman architecture built between 70 and 72 AD and supervised by the emperors Vespasian and Titus. In keeping with its impressive history, the term *coliseum* is now used to generically designate any large area in which one might witness a Monster Truck Challenge or a reunion concert by some band whose members you thought were already dead.

COLLEGE: A way for parents who cannot tell their children how they really feel to spend upward of a hundred grand to get them out of the house. Most parents are willing to do this, even though the return on the investment is nil, since their no-talent offspring spend four years studying nothing more than Jägermeister and wet T-shirt contests. Meanwhile, young people from other countries where they actually value education send their children over to get straight As. These industrious, hard-working immigrants then get all the good jobs while their hungover

The Official Dictionary of Sarcasm

American counterparts are using their BA in business management to keep their owner-operated Orange Julius franchise out of the red.

COLORING BOOK: An interim parenting tool, used to shut children up just after a meal and just before numbing them out with television.

COMEDIAN:
AN OPINIONATED LOUDMOUTH WHOM WE SO FEAR GETTING CORNERED BY AT A PARTY THAT WE WILL SHELL OUT A COVER CHARGE AND TWO-DRINK MINIMUM JUST TO ENSURE THAT THEY REMAIN BEHIND A MICROPHONE AT A SAFE DISTANCE FROM US AT ALL TIMES.

COMMANDING OFFICER: A person who is authorized to make a bunch of wrong-headed decisions on your behalf.

COMMANDMENTS, TEN: A list of suggestions for proper living delivered to Moses by God, which first introduced the rather enticing concepts of coveting your neighbor's wife and bearing false witness against your neighbor, two particularly satisfying things made all the more alluring when one is commanded not to do them.

COMMITMENT:

1. THE ACT OF BINDING ONESELF TO A SPECIFIC PATH—USUALLY AS REGARDS A RELATIONSHIP WITH A ROMANTIC PARTNER. 2. CONSIGNMENT TO A MENTAL HEALTH FACILITY. 3. THERE MAY BE NO DIFFERENCE BETWEEN 1 AND 2.

COMMITTEE: A group of supremely uninteresting people whose sole purpose is to gather together and make sure that nothing of note is ever accomplished.

COMMON COLD, THE:
SOMETHING GOD INFLICTS UPON HUMANS EVERY SO OFTEN TO GENTLY REMIND US THAT WE ARE 90 PERCENT SNOT.

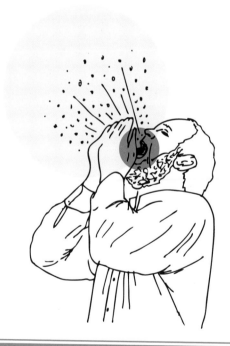

COMMUNICATION: 1. The act of conveying thoughts and ideas—rendered obsolete by marriage. 2. A completely useless college degree.

COMPANY: People who think it's OK to scarf down the meal you dropped a hundred bucks on and spent all day preparing just because they show up with a bottle of sparkling water.

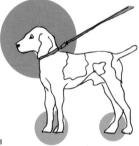

COMPATIBLE:

THE STATE OF BEING ABLE TO COEXIST CONGENIALLY. FOR HUMAN BEINGS, IT IS FAR MORE ACHIEVABLE WITH DOGS.

COMPETITION: The act of pitting one entity against another in a contest, with an eye toward determining a winner. The very foundation of a capitalist society, it ensures that those who are willing to work the hardest, sacrifice the most, and rise above those who would challenge their dominance will ultimately be rewarded by soon becoming a delicious meal for worms.

COMPUTER: Perhaps the most significant lifestyle-altering development of the past several hundred years, the computer allows us instant access to information and global communication as well as an unprecedented opportunity for community building and social activism. Which is why most of us use it to verify obscure song lyrics, get vital information on celebrities in rehab, and see which piano-playing cockatiel is getting the most hits this week.

CONFERENCE ROOM:

A ROOM SET ASIDE FOR MEETINGS IN THE WORKPLACE, COMMONLY FEATURING A LONG MAHOGANY TABLE, A DRY-ERASE BOARD, DAY-OLD DONUTS, AND MORE STIFLED YAWNS PER HOUR THAN AN INTRODUCTORY COURSE IN BYZANTINE HISTORY.

CONFUCIUS: Chinese philosopher born 551 BC. Known for his inspiring and humanistic quotations such as "Better a diamond with a flaw than a pebble without," "No matter where you go, there you are," and "I can't believe you morons think this crap is profound."

CONSERVATIVE: Someone who hates liberals because they have, at least once, seen themselves naked.

CONSOLE: To comfort in time of sorrow—usually in the hope that said comforting will help take her mind off the boyfriend who just dumped her and lead to tragic, tearful, but ultimately renewing sex.

CONSPIRACY THEORIST: Someone whom you indulged when they would go on a tirade about how the Air Force has a space alien hidden in a bunker somewhere—and to whom you gave polite audience as they maintained that the CIA killed JFK, Marilyn, and John Lennon—but who finally, totally, and irrevocably lost you when they started talking about how humanity is actually a race of freaking lizard people.

CONTRACTOR: A person who has the ability to make February turn into May, May into August, August into November, and so on.

CONVICT: Someone who has formulated a cunning plan to cheat, steal, or even kill to make the state take care of their food and lodging.

COPERNICUS, NICOLAUS:

FAMOUS SIXTEENTH-CENTURY ASTRONOMER NOTED FOR BEING THE FIRST TO POSIT THAT THE EARTH REVOLVES AROUND THE SUN. UNFORTUNATELY, HE NEVER LIVED TO SEE ALL THE PEOPLE WHO WERE BEATEN, STONED, IMPRISONED, AND EXCOMMUNICATED FOR ESPOUSING HIS BELIEFS.

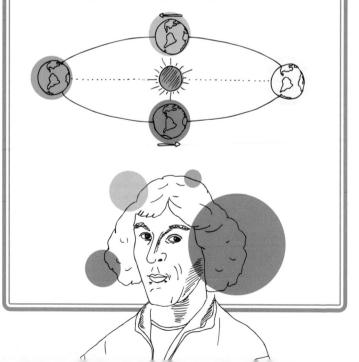

COSIGN: Banking industry slang for "when the hopeless deadbeat you were stupid enough to believe in defaults, we'll be in touch."

COSMETICS: Products without which the phrase "cheap whore" may never have come into existence.

COUGH: Something men are asked to do while a strange guy they barely know probes their testicles. OK, the strange guy is a medical professional, but still.

COUPLE: What nobody wants to admit they are until most of the damage has been done.

COWBOY: A profession marked by incredible dedication, an instinctive knowledge of both horses and cattle, punishing hours, and exposure to the elements. Makes you wonder how these guys keep from opening up a can of whoop-ass on bankers who have steer horns on the grille of their Silverado and who only get out of the truck to go line dancing. Not to mention a few wealthy ex-presidents who throw on a flannel shirt and a Stetson to try and convince people that they actually did a lick of real work on the ranches they left in the care of real cowboys, who knew what the hell they were doing.

The Official Dictionary of Sarcasm

COWORKER: A person who in any other circumstance you would go out of your way to avoid but whom you have gradually come to embrace as a friend—for no other reason than the fact that, like you, they are too inherently lazy to take any steps toward leaving a job they hate and are therefore happy to sit around and bitch about the place all day, also just like you. Should you ever muster the minimal effort it would take to actually hand in your walking papers, no way would you stay friends with such a loser.

COY: Pretending to be shy when one is actually flirting. Usually sends a mixed message to the opposite sex, so that they don't know whether to lunge at you and try to stick their tongue down your throat or lunge at you and try to stick their tongue down your throat and then apologize.

CPA: Certified public accountant. A three-letter acronym that just screams, "Do me, baby!"

CREDIT: A system that allows consumers to receive goods and services before paying for them in full. When extended by guys named Guido, the escalating and unreasonable rates of interest make the loan nearly impossible to ever pay off, resulting in shattered knee-caps or even death. When extended by multinational corporations, any difficulty in paying the equally reaming interest rates results in so many vicious, unfeeling calls from rabid telemarketers that you may find yourself begging for both shattered kneecaps and death.

CREDIT CARD: A small, wallet-sized device that finally made misery, ruin, and despair accessible to just about anyone.

CRUISE, TOM:

AN OUTWARDLY ATTRACTIVE BUT POSSIBLY MALEVOLENT ALIEN BEING, CLEVERLY SENT TO EARTH IN THE FORM OF A MOVIE STAR OF THE LATE TWENTIETH AND EARLY TWENTY-FIRST CENTURIES. WE SIMPLY AWAIT THE DAY WHEN HE RIPS OFF HIS FACE TO REVEAL THE INSECT-LIKE INTRUDER WITHIN WHILE EMITTING A DEAFENING, *BODY SNATCHERS*-LIKE HOWL. WITH THIS, HE WILL SUMMON THE FORCES OF HIS HOME PLANET AND LEAD THEM IN VANQUISHING THE UNGRATEFUL HUMANS WHO HAVE RIDICULED HIM FOR SO MANY YEARS.

CUBICLE:

A SMALL, SEMICONFINED WORKSTATION DESIGNED TO SUCK THE LIFE OUT OF ANYONE WHO INHABITS IT. THE STUPEFYING EFFECTS OF THESE AREAS MAY, IN SOME CASES, BE OFFSET BY TACKING A FEW DILBERT AND ZIGGY CARTOONS TO THE WALL OF THE CUBICLE WITH PUSHPINS. SIMILARLY, DISPLAYING PHOTOS OF YOUR FAVORITE SMALL CHILD OR PET COULD IN SOME CASES STAVE OFF FEELINGS OF UNEASE. IN THE END, HOWEVER, EVEN TREASURED IMAGES OF LOVED ONES OR A WITTY, ILLUSTRATED JAB AT THE FUTILITY OF ONE'S JOB ARE ONLY TEMPORARY MEASURES AND DO NOTHING MORE THAN ANNOY THOSE AROUND YOU, WHO FIND THEM NAUSEATINGLY CUTE AND WISH YOU WOULD TAKE THEM DOWN, DAMN IT.

CURIE, MARIE: Legendary scientist of Polish birth and French citizenship, Madame Curie was awarded two Nobel prizes for her accomplishments in discovering a few more elements that have the potential to freaking kill us all.

CURIOUS GEORGE: The children's book character that ushered in our lifelong love/hate relationship with pain in the ass, supposedly adorable, mischief-making cartoon simians.

CUSTOMER: A person who once came first and was always right, is now routinely ignored, disrespected, and even scoffed at by the clueless, text-messaging employees of most modern-day retail establishments. This has resulted in increased Internet commerce, wherein if the customer encounters a problem, he can simply phone a toll-free number to get ignored, disrespected, and even scoffed at.

CYBERSPACE: A place where well-off, thirty-ish, lantern-jawed men of international influence and tremendous sex appeal can post their profile to a dating site even though they are actually morbidly obese forty-nine-year-old science fiction fans who work on an assembly line processing animal entrails and live in their mother's basement.

The Official Dictionary of Sarcasm

CYCLOPS:

FIGURE OF GREEK MYTHOLOGY; A GIANT WITH A SINGLE EYE IN THE MIDDLE OF ITS FOREHEAD AND, CONSEQUENTLY, THE CRAPPIEST PERIPHERAL VISION KNOWN TO MAN. HOW THIS THING EVER GOT THE REPUTATION FOR BEING FORMIDABLE IS A MYSTERY, SINCE IT WAS PROBABLY EASIER TO SNEAK UP ON THAN A HEARING-IMPAIRED LABRADOR.

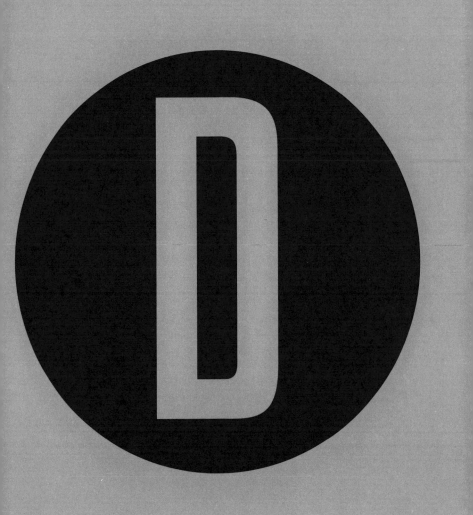

DALI, SALVADOR:

A TWENTIETH-CENTURY CATALONIAN ARTIST WHO CAME UP WITH STUFF LIKE MELTING CLOCKS AND HELPED USHER IN THE SURREALIST MOVEMENT, WHICH MAY HAVE BEEN RESPONSIBLE FOR THE FIRST WIDESPREAD USE OF THE PHRASE "WTF?"

DARE: A challenge put to someone, usually to attempt something risky. Most popularly used in the party game "Truth or Dare," which is really nothing more than a clever way to get someone you know to strip to their underwear or confess to having gotten to third base with someone widely thought to have a venereal disease.

DARWIN, CHARLES: Nineteenth-century British naturalist whose theory of natural selection and whose book *On the Origin of Species* put forth a theory of evolution that remains a source of controversy to this day, especially among obstinate, frightened morons.

DAUGHTER: One's female descendant. Fated to grow up and leave you for some worthless douche bag.

DA VINCI, LEONARDO: Some painter. Most likely named after that DiCaprio guy.

DEAN OF STUDENTS: A person trained to be endlessly patient with pathological liars.

DEATH: AN INCREDIBLE OPPORTUNITY TO LEAVE YOUR MASSIVE, FLOOR-TO-CEILING COLLECTION OF WORTHLESS VINYL LPS FOR SOMEONE ELSE TO DEAL WITH.

DEBATE: 1. A formal argument or dialogue, often between opposing-party politicians, in which one person mentions a lot of things he or she supposedly stands for that will immediately be forgotten once in office, and everyone else disagrees with this learned colleague on a point-by-point basis, even though it doesn't matter because, as mentioned, none of these entrenched media whores are capable of uttering one shred of truth in the first place. 2. A club in high school joined by those who need to have a few hours a day wherein they aren't getting beaten up.

DEBT:

SOMETHING YOU NEVER NOTICE UNTIL IT GETS UP TO YOUR EYEBALLS.

DECAF: Coffee that doesn't work.

DEGREE: A certificate of academic achievement awarded at the college level. Comes in very handy when asking people if they want fries with that.

DELETE: A key that, when smacked angrily and repeatedly along with CTRL and ALT, provides the illusion that once your computer has frozen you can fix it by . . . arrggghh! Stupid piece of worthless crap—arrggghhh—arrggghhh—hate you—hate you—*%@!&#—come on!—damn it—come on!—arrggghhh—arrggghh!!!! Forget it, just forget it!!!

DE NIRO, ROBERT: Famous twentieth-century film actor who is right bloody sick of people coming up to him and going, "You talkin' to me?"

DENTAL HYGIENIST: The sexiest person you will ever spit a mouthful of your bloody saliva into a suction sink in front of.

DENTIST: A person to whom you provide boat payments as a way of thanking them for sending a shooting pain through your entire central nervous system.

DEODORANT: A product that always manages to suddenly lose its effectiveness on a crowded subway, during a job interview, or just as one is attempting foreplay with a new partner.

DEODORIZER:
A MIST OR AEROSOL SPRAYED INTO THE AIR IN THE FUTILE HOPE THAT A LOVELY LAVENDER-CITRUS SCENT MIGHT SOMEHOW OVERCOME THE PERSISTENT AROMA OF ONE OF YOUR ROOMMATE'S TOXIC TOILET DEPOSITS.

DEPENDENT: One who must rely on someone else for support. See also: *musician.*

DESIRE: A longing or passion for something or someone. May include sheep in certain dire circumstances.

DESK: Something on the top of which you have always wanted to have fierce, animalistic sex with your coworker, but somehow only ever manage to use for data entry and the occasional power-stapling job.

DESPAIR: An utter loss of hope; a feeling of uselessness. Often brought about through contact with a greeter at Wal-Mart.

DESSERT: God's way of making the clogging of your arteries extremely delicious.

DETERMINED: About to fail.

DEVOUT: Constantly horny.

DIAMOND:

A PRECIOUS GEMSTONE USED IN JEWELRY AND COMMONLY MINED IN WAR-TORN REGIONS OF THE WORLD, WHERE A TRAIL OF ILLEGAL ARMS AND DEATH FOLLOW IN ITS WAKE. NOW THEN, WHERE WAS I . . . OH, YEAH, WILL YOU MARRY ME?

DICKENS, CHARLES:
THE MAN RESPONSIBLE FOR EVERY LOUSY COMMUNITY-THEATER PRODUCTION OF *A CHRISTMAS CAROL* YOU HAVE EVER HAD TO SIT THROUGH BECAUSE YOUR WIFE HAD A FRIEND FROM WORK WHO WAS PLAYING BOB CRATCHIT.

DICTATOR: A tyrannical ruler. Some people who have been labeled as dictators throughout history include Mussolini, Stalin, and parents who even remotely suggest that their child might want to do less text messaging.

DICTIONARY: A reference book that provides definitions of various words or provides a companion text illuminating what those words mean in another language. *The Attorney-to-English Dictionary* and the *World of Warcraft-to-English Dictionary* are two volumes particularly crucial in helping to grasp what the hell these people are talking about.

DIET:

A STRICT REGIMEN CONCERNING THE INTAKE OF FOOD, CONSCIENTIOUSLY OBSERVED FOR APPROXIMATELY FOUR AND A HALF DAYS, AT WHICH POINT YOU REALIZE YOU'RE OK WITH BEING FAT.

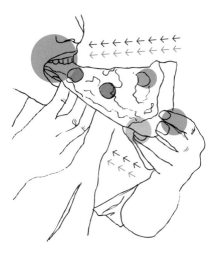

DIFFERENT: Not the same; unique unto itself. In a constantly progressing society, the standards for what constitutes *different* change frequently. However, that construction worker who moonlights as Judy Garland—that's different. And someone letting you into traffic—that's definitely different.

DIFFICULT:
NOT WORTH TRYING.

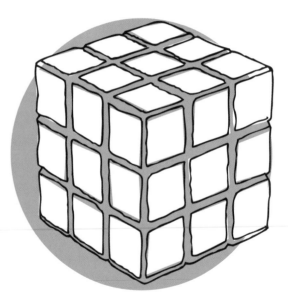

DIPLOMATIC: Tactful; sensitive to interpersonal situations—that is, unable to call someone a dick no matter how richly they deserve it.

DIRTY: A state of being unclean. Can also refer to an emotionally dirty state, such as the tainted way one might feel after betraying a friend, joining in the malicious ridicule of another human being, or watching *Saw*.

DISC JOCKEY (DEEJAY):

ONE OF THE MANY IRREPRESSIBLE RESIDENTS OF VARIOUS MORNING "ZOOS" ACROSS THE NATION, YOUR LOCAL DISC JOCKEY IS A ZANY, IRREVERENT MOTORMOUTH WHOSE GIGGLING, ADOLESCENT CADENCES AND OBNOXIOUS, SCREAMING INTERACTIONS WITH GUESTS AND CALLERS ALIKE HAVE BEEN SCIENTIFICALLY PROVEN TO CAUSE BLEEDING IN THE EARS AFTER LESS THAN FIVE MINUTES OF EXPOSURE. ONE CAN ONLY IMAGINE WHAT THE HOME LIFE OF THESE IN-YOUR-FACE BUFFOONS MUST BE LIKE, ALTHOUGH THE BREAKFAST TABLE PROBABLY FEATURES A LONG-SUFFERING SIGNIFICANT OTHER HAVING TO ENDURE A FUSILLADE OF LAME-ASS JOKES, EACH ONE PUNCTUATED BY THE SQUEEZING OF A BICYCLE HORN.

The Official Dictionary of Sarcasm

DISCREET: Capable of showing restraint in the public discussion of private matters. And when it comes to the grunting sounds you heard emanating from the boss's office last week, stretching out that restraint over as long as it takes for the affair to be over could provide you with a sizable second-income stream.

DISCUSSION: A lengthy exchange of ideas around a given topic. And a total pain in the ass.

DISGRUNTLED: Way too kind a word for a freaking nut job who shows up to work with an Uzi.

DISNEYLAND: An excruciating journey into a relentlessly upbeat world that shovels ridiculous, impractical fairy tale fantasies into the minds of children, failing utterly to prepare the impressionable youngsters for the fact that none of this crap can ever come true in the real world. The entire gigantic lie of an experience is made all the more galling by an admission fee that could supply rice to an impoverished nation for an entire fiscal year; unbearably long lines of sticky children and their utterly depleted guardians waiting to take in a three-and-a-half-minute ride through a dank, shadowy interior punctuated by the occasional hologram; and restaurants with all of four items on the menu, none of which is cheaper than $21.95. Add to this the unsettling figures of strolling, big-headed, eerily nonspeaking cartoon characters, and it isn't long before you realize you have just spent the day wandering around inside the unchecked id of a man who reportedly had his corpse frozen.

DISNEYWORLD: See previous entry, add humidity.

DIVORCE: An eventuality that will soon be included as part of the marriage vows.

DOCTOR: 1. A person who trained anywhere from eight to twelve years in order that you would wait something very close to that span of time while sitting alone on a gurney wearing nothing but a paper gown and freezing your semiexposed buttocks off. 2. Any of the above-named profession, who, after keeping you waiting for what seems like the aforementioned twelve-year period, are also determined to spend no more than from thirty to forty-five seconds with you, declaring a diagnosis of anything from bronchitis to lymphoma in the same dispassionate monotone before telling you to put your clothes back and then writing out a scrip in Sanskrit.

DOCUMENTARY: A movie without any good parts.

DOG: A creature to which history attributes the noble qualities of being there to rescue you from a raging river but who, in reality, would probably sit dozing, chin on paws, while you drown in quicksand and who would forget your very existence in a nanosecond if someone else got to him with some Alpo before you did.

DOMAIN NAME: Something you are quick to shell out a hundred dollars a year for so that no one else on the Internet can snag it, never stopping to think that www. MyNameIsPeteAndIReallyLike1950sLithuanianSpyMovie Memorabilia.com may not exactly start a bidding war.

DOUGHNUT:

A FOOD CREATED IN RESPONSE TO THE NOTION THAT IF SOMETHING HAS 20 GRAMS OF SUGAR, 25 GRAMS OF FAT, AND 425 CALORIES, THEN IT SHOULD BE MADE AVAILABLE IN GROUPS OF TWELVE.

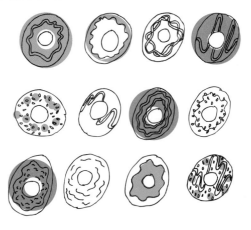

The Official Dictionary of Sarcasm

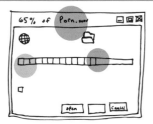

DOWNLOAD: THE TRANSFER OF DATA (PORN) FROM THE COMPUTER OF THE (PORN) HOST TO THE PERSONAL COMPUTER OF THE (PORN) USER.

DRAGON: Mythological fire-breathing creature with a giant serpent's body and the claws of a lion. It is often depicted as being the obstacle between a brave knight and a damsel in distress, proving that even in medieval times, they needed a cagey metaphor for the kind of hell a man will go through for a shot at some tail.

DRAMA: 1. A theatrical presentation of a written work. 2. What your last three relationships could have used a lot less of.

DRESS: Something that does not, I said *not*, make you look fat.

DRUGS: Substances used for the treatment of any of various conditions, and whose minimal side effects include bloating, cramps, dizziness, constipation, disorientation, leaking, partial blindness, partial paralysis, cancer, possible death, and dry mouth.

DRUMMER: A person who hangs around with musicians.

DRUNK: Intoxicated with alcoholic beverages. An absolutely crucial component in the decision to photocopy one's ass cheeks.

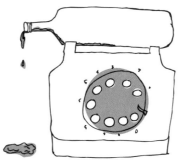

DRUNK DIALING:

THE VAIN HOPE THAT SLURRING YOUR WORDS OVER A CELL PHONE AT THREE–THIRTY IN THE MORNING WILL CONVINCE THE PERSON WHO DUMPED YOU SIX YEARS AGO TO SUDDENLY WANT YOU WAY BAD.

DRY: A type of wit that employs an understated and sardonic tone. Often associated with droll British people, dry wit usually involves phrases like, "I say, Nigel, that cricket bat is ever so scrummy" and is funny to approximately six people, five of whom will soon be dead.

DRYER: A device that has been incrementally lowering the amount of time you get for twenty-five cents until it's, like, two minutes or something, necessitating the insertion of close to nine dollars' worth of quarters just to make sure you don't go home with damp elastic in all of your underwear.

DUCT TAPE: A product that would probably be employed as a freaking yurt or a damn chastity belt before it is ever actually used on a freaking duct.

DUI: Dvrinig udner the iflnuence. Also: DWI, divring wilhe ixtonicated.

DYLAN, BOB:
MUSIC INDUSTRY LEGEND KNOWN FOR HIS SOCIOPOLITICAL FOLK SONGS OF THE 1960S AND FOR WINNING A LATE-TWENTIETH-CENTURY GRAMMY AWARD IN THE CATEGORY OF "GUY WHO SOUNDS MOST LIKE A HAMSTER WOULD SOUND IF A HAMSTER COULD, IN FACT, SING."

DYSFUNCTIONAL: Impaired in some way, often as regards the family unit. A term much overused by a whole generation of the self-absorbed middle class, who seem to have no qualms about looking a deeply scarred abuse survivor in the face and saying that they, too, grew up in a dysfunctional family because mom and dad never gave them the emotional permission to realize their own uniqueness. It's all Oprah's fault.

EARTH: Third planet from the sun, inhabited by millions of complex and interesting life forms, and humans.

EASTER BUNNY:

AN IMAGINARY CREATURE WHOSE FLOPPY EARS, UNGAINLY FEET, AND WICKER BASKET FULL OF PAINTED EGGS SOMEHOW CAME TO SYMBOLIZE THE DEATH AND RESURRECTION OF JESUS CHRIST.

EASY: A term used by both men and women to express contempt for a woman who has a lot more sex than they could ever dream of having.

EATING: The part of your day that commonly occurs between sleeping and taking a dump.

ECCENTRIC: The type of unconventional, idiosyncratic, oddball character with whom it is utterly unbearable to spend even five minutes in the same room, but whom we somehow find uplifting and inspiring when they are the fictional subject of a two-hour movie.

E-COMMERCE: A convenient way to make your bank account accessible to criminals without having to leave the comfort and safety of your own home.

The Official Dictionary of Sarcasm

ECONOMY: A system of commerce in which a small group of people who actually care about such things move massive amounts of imaginary money around on imaginary tote boards while the rest of us go to work, get the occasional oil change, and buy entire seasons of television programs in boxed sets.

EDGY: An otherwise normal person or work of art deemed provocative or daring by virtue of a little profanity, self-mutilation, or both.

EDISON, THOMAS: American businessman active in the late nineteenth and early twentieth centuries. Edison either invented or was instrumental in pioneering electric light, the telephone, and motion pictures, ensuring that generations to come would have more efficient ways to see, communicate with, and preserve memories of people they cannot stand.

EDUCATION: Sumthing that ewsed tu one tyme be valewed in the U.S. of Amurica, butt now iz not so mutch annymor.

EFFEMINATE: A term rendered obsolete by the word *metrosexual*.

EGO: The part of one's mind that contains awareness and the sense of one's own individuality. Highly developed in actors, models, sports figures, doctors, real estate tycoons, and, God help us, our children.

EIFFEL TOWER, THE: Completed in Paris in 1889, this 1,062-foot-tall monument went up during that time when a bunch of guys kept building bigger and bigger phallic symbols to overcompensate for deeply repressed feelings of inadequacy.

EIGHTEEN WHEELER:
A TRACTOR TRAILER TRUCK THAT IS THE SUBJECT OF MANY A SONG AND THE CAUSE OF MANY A HEMORRHOID.

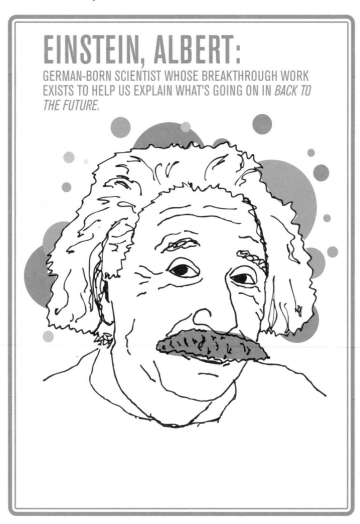

EINSTEIN, ALBERT:
GERMAN-BORN SCIENTIST WHOSE BREAKTHROUGH WORK EXISTS TO HELP US EXPLAIN WHAT'S GOING ON IN *BACK TO THE FUTURE.*

ELDERLY: Of advanced years. Or, as it is known in the entertainment industry, twenty-seven.

ELECTION: An ongoing part of the democratic process in which politicians and the post office team up to make sure American citizens have enough leaflets.

ELEVATOR: A conveyance designed to induce awkward silences whenever more than one person occupies it at the same time.

ELLIS ISLAND: Established as a national monument in 1965, this port of entry located in New York Harbor has attained a special romanticized sheen in history, mostly because from 1892 to 1954, it served as the main gateway for the good, nice, light-skinned immigrants.

E-MAIL: A system for the sending of messages over a computer network, its chief purpose is to give otherwise dull people the opportunity to create obtuse and impenetrable e-mail addresses that reflect sensibilities none of their friends ever knew they possessed. Such offerings as "wombatfan39" or "deathobsessedEvan" are meant to convey individuality, but only succeed in creeping us out.

EMASCULATE: To lessen virility or the perception of virility. One of the easiest things in the world to accomplish: a man can be emasculated by anything from a simple roll of the eyes to the more complicated "Why don't you just send the food back if you don't like it?" gambit.

EMBALMING:

THE CHEMICAL TREATMENT OF A CORPSE TO FORESTALL ITS DECAY. USED REGULARLY ON LARRY KING.

EMERGENCY ROOM: A place where you are predisposed to be grateful for any medical care you receive, given that after sitting doubled-over in pain for nine hours in a room full of bleeding gunshot-wound victims and vibrating tubercular cases coughing their contagions directly into your face, you wish you were dead anyway.

EMOTICON: A computer-keyboard-generated symbol employed to express an emotion in a typed message. For example, a smiley face assembled from a colon, dash, and right parentheses is commonly used to communicate the phrase "I understand that the somewhat hostile phrase I just typed could be interpreted to mean that I think you're an amoral scuz bucket who is probably a public masturbator, so I am adding this little smile to make you think that I don't really mean that, even though I do."

EMPOWERMENT: The feeling of being imbued with a sense of one's own power. A bogus concept popularized by self-help gurus whose best-selling books generate enough profits to give them empowerment up the yin yang.

EMPTY: Having a state of nothingness or lacking in meaning—as such, the best sex you will ever have.

ENABLING: In psychology, a term meaning the tacit allowing of an ongoing negative behavior in another person. In real life, a term meaning "wanker."

ENDANGERED SPECIES: An organism that faces the risk of becoming extinct. Among the most widely known endangered species are the Siberian tiger, the blue whale, and people who still have a landline.

ENGAGEMENT:

AN ANCIENT AND BIZARRE PACT OF IMPENDING CONNUBIAL COMMITMENT, THIS STRANGE RITUAL CAUSES MEN AND WOMEN ALIKE TO SUDDENLY COMPILE A WISH LIST OF MORE KITCHEN UTENSILS AND BATH TOWEL SETS THAN THEY COULD EVER POSSIBLY USE.

ENGLISH: A language in which most Bangalore-based tech support people are more fluent than most of the pissed-off semiliterate people who call them from America.

ENLIGHTENMENT: A deeper, more transcendent understanding of life that usually hits about a quarter of a second before you croak.

ENOUGH:

1. AN AMOUNT THAT IS SUFFICIENT TO ONE'S NEEDS. SOMETHING AMERICANS ALWAYS RESOLVE TO STICK TO AFTER SEEING A PROGRAM ON UNDERDEVELOPED COUNTRIES RAVAGED BY POVERTY AND MALNUTRITION, BUT THAT THEY SOON FORGET WHEN THAT MOVIE THEY ALREADY HAVE ON VHS AND DVD FINALLY GETS RELEASED ON BLU-RAY. 2. WHAT PARENTS YELL INTO THE GARAGE AFTER THREE HOURS OF DRUM PRACTICE.

ENTERTAINMENT: Something we keep trying to convince ourselves *Saturday Night Live* is.

ENTREPRENEUR: A much-abused term, it can mean either a visionary businessperson who takes on the enormous risk of setting up a bold new venture or someone who shuffles around their studio apartment openly scratching themselves through their half-open bathrobe, earning just enough to buy SpaghettiO's and toilet paper by gradually selling off their action figure collection on eBay.

ENVY: A spiteful feeling brought on by resentment of another's possessions or achievements. Traditionally experienced at three key stages of the human life. First, when contemplating how much better the most popular person in high school has it than you; second, when seeing images of the famous and powerful on television and realizing your shot at joining them is over; and third, when discovering that you are the only one in your age group who has to get up three times a night to pee.

EQUALITY: The noble principle of fairness and equal representation for all, as evidenced on television by the fact that Hispanic people get to play all the domestics, African Americans get to play all the gangbangers, and Asians get to play all the convenience store owners.

ERASER:

SOMETHING THAT IS CALLED A RUBBER IN ENGLAND, WHICH IS ALWAYS GOOD FOR A CHUCKLE.

EROTIC: Titillating, causing arousal. In other words, all the things you have to picture to look like you're enjoying it with someone who would never let you do the things you're picturing.

ESCORT: A job that allows men all the convenience of being a prostitute without having to get all tarted up like their skanky streetwalker cousins.

ESTEEMED:

SLANG. AN IDIOT. "WELCOME TO THE PODIUM PLEASE, OUR ESTEEMED REGIONAL MANAGING DIRECTOR!"

ESTRANGED: Polite word for a complete dick who you never want to see again.

ETHEREAL: Possessing a celestial or otherworldly quality; often exhibited by women who wear more than one scarf over a loose-fitting caftan, claim to be able to draw down the moon to serve their will, and usually have a cat that looks like it probably took great pleasure in castrating the last five men who dared step inside the pentagram.

EUROPE: A place where many local, non-English-speaking residents will probably understand what it is you are trying to ask them if you ask it a second time, only much louder.

EXACERBATE: A word that sounds so much like another, more objectionable word that it is a good thing not too many people know how to use it in a sentence.

EXCEL: Confounding Microsoft spreadsheet application designed by a very cruel person who clearly wants a large percentage of its users to have an embolism.

EXECUTIVE: A distinction given to certain bathrooms, denoting that those allowed into them are, unlike the rest of us, able to produce defecations that smell like a fragrant field of flowers.

EXERCISE: Walking from one's front door to one's car.

EXISTENCE: A Latin word meaning "endless, mind-numbing grind."

EXPECTATIONS: The things our parents have for us that compel us to go to a good school and get a law degree instead of realizing that all we ever really wanted to do was backpack through Asia Minor for the rest of our lives and then oversee an alpaca farm.

EXPERIENCE:
THE SECTION OF A RÉSUMÉ THAT FEATURES COMPLETE AND UTTER BULLSHIT.

EXPERIMENTAL: Workplace-speak for "this will never work but they're making us try it, so just be patient, and in a few weeks they will scrap it and we can all return to our normal levels of uninterest and inefficiency."

EXPERT: A person who gets to give an opinion via satellite on television news programs simply because he is an adjunct professor of public health policy at Sunnydale Community College and wrote a book called something like *World Perspectives on the Indigenous Growth of Interdepartmental Conflict in Tanzania, 1929–1947.*

EXPLOITATION: Perfectly good entertainment given a bad name by boring morons.

The Official Dictionary of Sarcasm

EXTREME:
A WORD USED AS A PREFIX TO IMPLY THAT EVERYTHING FROM YOUR ENERGY BAR TO YOUR FACIAL TISSUE IS THAT MUCH MORE KICK-ASS.

FABULOUS: A superlative that straight men should just admit they have been using for more years than they care to admit.

FACEBOOK:

AN INTERNET DESTINATION FOR PEOPLE WHO WANT TO BE FOUND BY EVERYONE WHO USED TO BEAT THEM UP IN HIGH SCHOOL.

FACE TIME: The absolute last resort after trying to avoid personal contact with a moron by texting, e-mail, or cell phone has failed.

FACETIOUS: Tongue-in-cheek; humorous observation made in contrast to the seriousness of the situation. *"Gee, sorry your dad is dead, but now you won't have to pay him back for college!"*

FACTS: Things that are unnecessary in the success of politicians, Fox News commentators, and Scientologists.

FAIR:
1. A ONCE-IN-A-LIFETIME OPPORTUNITY TO SEE A HOG-JUDGING CONTEST AND CONSUME FRIED CHEESE IN THE SAME LOCATION. 2. WHAT LIFE NEVER IS, SO SUCK IT UP AND DEAL WITH IT.

FAITH: A deeply personal, spiritual set of beliefs that provides for the option of engaging in endless, bloody civil war with anyone who has a different set of deeply personal, spiritual beliefs than you.

FALL: A magical time of year, during which the leaves provide a splash of brilliant color before falling to the ground dead, in an ominous foreshadowing of the frigid, metaphorical death that awaits us all from now until Daylight Saving Time.

FALLIBLE: What you are praying that most store-bought pregnancy tests often are.

FAMILY: A group of people you spend eighteen years having dinner with every night before realizing you have plenty of better things to do.

FAMOUS: A state of being widely known, which most of us do not have the talent or societal status to achieve, although there are opportunities to achieve notoriety if one is lucky enough to have slept with one's seventh-grade student, had one's penis lopped off by an angry lover, or received the good fortune of being caught and convicted for a string of heinous and brutal murders.

FAN:
A STALKER WAITING TO HAPPEN.

FAQ: Frequently asked questions. Neither questions nor frequently asked, this is the section of the Web site that compiles all the spin a company wants to snowball you with in one convenient location. It usually features such noninquiries as "Can I Pay with a Credit Card?" (to which the answer is—duh—"yes"), and "What Is the Preferred Customer Discount Plan?" (to which the answer is—duh—"an opportunity for us to assist you in hemorrhaging money").

FARMER: A person who receives government subsidies to pretend that he doesn't exist so that people everywhere are free to assume that bins and bins full of oranges and potatoes fall from the sky into our supermarkets each and every day.

FASHION: Something that a total of six people actually have time to follow. Which might explain why we keep seeing clips of runway models wearing some of the weirdest crap in the world, none of which ever makes it to your local Target.

FAT: What you don't realize you are getting until you have to suck in your gut even when you are lying down.

FATHER: 1. The male parent; in Western cultures, he is a nonentity who is expected to sit back and take it from spouse and children alike. 2. A term of respect for the person who might be molesting the altar boy.

FEAR: Anxiety or dread caused by the certainty that something terrible is about to happen, such as when walking alone down a dark alley or heading home for Thanksgiving.

FEELINGS: SOMETHING YOU DIDN'T KNOW YOU HAD UNTIL YOU CRIED AT THE END OF *ROCKY*.

FEISTY: A word that is now no longer used except as a prefix to the phrase *old broad*.

FEMALE: A person whose ability to generate human life pisses men off to such an extent that men decided to pay them anywhere from 5 to 25 percent less for doing the same job they do.

FEMALE IMPERSONATOR: Someone you found very attractive and even began to have elaborate sexual fantasies about before your friend told you the truth and you just about hurled.

FEMININE: Characteristic of women. Called to mind by such items as potpourri, fine lace, toilet paper cozies, and the ability to stick the knife in just when you are at your most vulnerable, sometimes even in front of your damn friends.

FIDGETY: What you call a child who cannot sit still before abdicating yourself of all responsibility for their condition and getting someone to give them Ritalin.

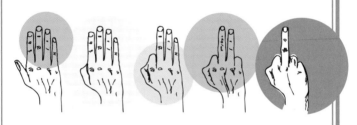

FINGER, THE:
SOMETHING YOU GIVE TO OTHER HUMAN BEINGS WHEN YOU CANNOT FIND THE RIGHT WORDS TO SAY EXACTLY HOW MUCH THEIR VERY EXISTENCE HAS SO DEEPLY IMPACTED YOUR LIFE.

FIRED: Something you lie awake nights hoping you will be because you don't have the balls to quit.

FIREMAN: A person who spends most of the day playing cards and petting a Dalmatian, yet who gets to do something so totally badass when he actually *does* work that he is guaranteed sex for the rest of his life.

FIRST CLASS:
A POSTAL CLASSIFICATION THAT ASSURES YOUR MAIL WILL BE LOST EVEN SOONER THAN IF SENT IT AT THE REGULAR RATE.

FISH: Any of various aquatic vertebrates that cannot fathom why people only associate them with white wine, when in fact they would probably be equally tasty when served with red.

FISHING:
ONE OF THE RISKIEST SPORTS IN EXISTENCE, FISHING PITS A MONSTROUS, IMPOSING BEAST WITH NO ARMS AND LEGS AGAINST MEN SITTING IN A BOAT

TWENTY TIMES THE SIZE OF THEIR ADVERSARY, DRINKING BEER OUT OF A STYROFOAM COOLER, AND TELLING BLONDE JOKES WHILE WAITING FOR THEIR PREY TO SWIM ONTO A SHARPLY POINTED HOOK AND DIE.

FLAG: A symbol of national allegiance, now available in magnet form so that if you ever decide you're not that hot on your country after all, you can simply take it off and replace it with a funny quote from *Napoleon Dynamite*.

FLIGHT ATTENDANT:

A PERSON WHO SPEAKS UNINTELLIGIBLY INTO A DISTORTED PA SYSTEM IN BETWEEN OPENING CANS OF COKE AND SITTING THROUGH THAT GALLING VIDEO OF THE SAFETY DEMONSTRATION, WHICH USED TO BE PERFORMED LIVE, COMPLETE WITH THE SEAT BELT CLICKING INTO PLACE AND THE OXYGEN MASKS AND BLOWING INTO THE LIFE PRESERVER TUBES AND EVERYTHING.

FLOWERS:

A HOLLOW GESTURE OF APOLOGY MADE ALL THE MORE HOLLOW BY THE FACT THAT YOU ORDERED THEM ONLINE.

FOOLISH: Exhibiting stupidity or judgment so unsound as to be almost laughable.

FOOTBALL:

1. AN AMERICAN SPORT IN WHICH MEN TRY TO GET A TEARDROP-SHAPED BALL FROM ONE END OF A BIG FIELD TO ANOTHER WHILE GRUNTING, PILING ON TOP OF ONE ANOTHER, AND GIDDILY JUMPING UP AND DOWN WHEN THEY SUCCEED. HOMOEROTIC? YOU DECIDE. 2. AN ENGLISH SPORT IN WHICH THE FANS COULD KICK THE ASS OF JUST ABOUT ANY OF THE PLAYERS.

FORD, HENRY:
PIONEERING AUTO MANUFACTURER WHO PROVED THAT WITH A LITTLE SWEAT, HARD WORK, AND DETERMINATION, YOU CAN ONE DAY HAVE A GOOD PERCENTAGE OF YOUR AMERICAN CAR ASSEMBLED BY PEOPLE IN TOKYO.

FOREPLAY: Two minutes of boring displays of affection that must be endured if you want to get to the good stuff.

FORGIVE: To cease assigning blame or anger to another in a given situation. Absolutely far less fun than holding on to bitter resentment for a lifetime and taking your righteous fury to the grave.

FRANCE: A country that inspires an almost pathological contempt in Americans who, much to their dismay, cannot eat all the freaking Brie they want and still not gain any weight.

FREUD, SIGMUND: Austrian founder of psychoanalysis. We have this guy to thank for making that perfectly nice dream about our mother, Catherine Zeta-Jones, and a persimmon seem somehow dirty.

FRIEND: A person you use to pass the time between relationships.

FRUIT: Literally, the ripened ovaries of a seed plant. Gross. No wonder you don't eat as much of it as you should.

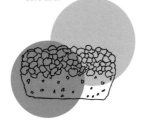

FRUITCAKE:
A GIFT GIVEN TO YOU LAST CHRISTMAS BY PEOPLE WHO SHREWDLY ANTICIPATED YOUR NEEDING A DOORSTOP THIS CHRISTMAS.

FUNKY: What Republicans think Celine Dion is.

FUN-LOVING: While on a deeper level this phrase can indicate a person who acts out in public to cope with an intense amount of inner pain, all you really need to know is that you're dealing with someone who will drop their drawers at the slightest provocation.

GALILEO: Astronomer and physicist often called the father of modern science. Although he was condemned and imprisoned by the Roman authority for his forward-thinking view of the structure of the universe, he did, many years later, end up as part of a song lyric in *Bohemian Rhapsody* by Queen, so hopefully that makes up for it.

GANDHI, MAHATMA: A man who must have done something pretty important, or Ben Kingsley would never have played him in a movie.

GANGSTA: Street slang for a member of a gang, growing out of the violent conflict engendered by the poverty and class struggle that erupts in economically underprivileged African American urban neighborhoods. Twenty minutes later, the term was co-opted by suburban white kids, who flash gang signs and wear baggy jeans and backward baseball caps to express their anger over a system that is designed to give them every advantage in life.

GARAGE: A place where a man keeps a wall-mounted rack of unused tools, a rusty miter box, and a table-mounted vise so that he can claim to have a "workshop" to go to when he has just had an argument with his wife.

GASOLINE:
AN UNREGULATED FORM OF CRACK USED WITH IMPUNITY BY EVERYONE IN THE FREE WORLD.

GAY: Something that a healthy acknowledgment of how stunningly handsome George Clooney is does not necessarily make you.

GEEK: Either someone who bites the heads off chickens or anyone who is inordinately obsessed by a particular area of interest (such as *computer geek*, *comic book geek*, or *sports geek*). It is unclear how the term evolved from one used to describe a weird, tragic, repulsive social deviant to one used to describe someone who . . . Oh, never mind, it makes sense after all.

GENGHIS KHAN: Thirteenth-century leader of the Mongol Horde. Or, as the position is known today: mall security.

GENIUS: 1. Exceptional, often unheard-of intellectual ability. Traditionally a grossly overused compliment; since these days it is often applied to Einstein and Quentin Tarantino in the same breath, it is safe to say it has been rendered devoid of any meaning. 2. Use of the term with an arched eyebrow insinuates that the person one is addressing has an IQ somewhere south of the common housefly. Obvious choices for such derision would include Jessica Simpson, Charo, or anyone from the second Bush administration.

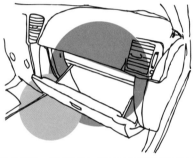

GLOVE COMPARTMENT:

A SMALL AUTOMOBILE-DASHBOARD CONTAINER THAT HAS NEVER ACTUALLY BEEN USED AS A RECEPTACLE FOR ITS NAMESAKE. HOWEVER, THE ALTERNATIVE TERM *LICENSE, REGISTRATION, AND PROOF-OF-INSURANCE COMPARTMENT* WAS REJECTED ON THE BASIS OF AWKWARDNESS, WHILE *HANDGUN COMPARTMENT* WAS PASSED OVER FOR MORE OBVIOUS REASONS.

GOD: Someone whose very clever lawyers came up with the "individual free will" clause to make sure their holier-than-thou client could never be held accountable for a single damn thing.

GOLDFISH:
A CREATURE SPECIALLY BRED TO PROVIDE YOUNG CHILDREN EARLY TRAINING IN FLUSHING SOMETHING DEAD DOWN THE TOILET.

GOLF: A so-called sport whose strolling, lackadaisical participants are so unaccustomed to the consequences of physical exertion that all eighteen of their playing areas include a place to wash their balls.

GOOGLE: Internet search engine whose sole function is to redirect you to Wikipedia, which is where you should have started anyway.

GOSSIP: Indulging in malicious rumor-mongering, commonly in the workplace, which could potentially ruin the reputation and job security of a fellow employee. And man, it just doesn't get any better than that.

GOVERNMENT: A giant, mutated organism that occupies one or more old buildings in any given city, secreting useless waste product derived from taxpayer contributions and pulling from its butt an endless stream of forms that need filling out in triplicate.

GPS:

GLOBAL POSITIONING SYSTEM. A COMPUTERIZED SATELLITE NAVIGATION PROGRAM NOW USED WIDELY IN AUTOMOBILES BY PEOPLE WHO, AMAZINGLY, ARE NOT CREEPED OUT BY THE FACT THAT A SATELLITE SOMEWHERE NOT ONLY KNOWS EXACTLY WHERE THEY ARE BUT SPEAKS UP WHEN THEY NEED TO MAKE A LEFT.

GRAND CANYON, THE: A gorge in Arizona that is a mile deep, eighteen miles wide, and almost three hundred miles long. Its awe-inspiring natural beauty cannot help but take one's breath away for a few minutes before moving on to see the much more stimulating *Blue Man Group* in nearby Las Vegas.

GRANDPARENTS: A couple of old farts who have decided to give you all the unconditional love they quite obviously withheld from your parents.

GREAT WALL OF CHINA: A remarkable testament to what several million slaves can accomplish when an emperor puts his mind to it.

GREEN: A catch-all term meaning "environmentally friendly," it allows Subaru-driving yuppies to get all high and mighty about how they are single-handedly saving the planet by not getting paper statements for their credit cards.

GROUNDHOG DAY:
OBSERVED ON FEBRUARY 2 OF EACH YEAR, THIS IS A DAY DEDICATED TO THE DEEP-SEATED AMERICAN BELIEF THAT A CAPTIVE RODENT IS CAPABLE OF PREDICTING THE WEATHER.

GUILT: A feeling of compunction, caused by the often unfounded certainty that one is to blame for something that has gone wrong. Among those of the Jewish and Roman Catholic faiths, this condition persists from birth until death. In the former religion, it is brought about by the nagging feeling that one has shamed one's parents; in the latter religion, it is brought about by the nagging feeling that dead people can see you masturbating.

GUITAR, ACOUSTIC:

A STRINGED INSTRUMENT THAT CAN TRANSFORM AN UNATTRACTIVE PERSON WHO HAS BEEN UNABLE TO GAIN POPULARITY BY EXCELLING AT SPORTS INTO A DYLANESQUE, SANDAL-WEARING DEEP THINKER WHO SUDDENLY HAS MORE HIPPIE-CHICKS WANTING TO SLEEP WITH HIM THAN HE COULD EVER POSSIBLY HANDLE.

GUITAR, ELECTRIC: A string instrument amplified electronically that can transform an unattractive person who has been unable to gain popularity by excelling at sports into a Van Halenesque tongue wiggler with leather pants who suddenly has more skanks wanting to sleep with him than he could ever possibly handle.

GUN: A prop without which 99.9 percent of all Hollywood movies would have no idea how to end.

GUTENBERG, JOHANNES: Fifteenth-century printer who originated the mass production of moveable type. If someone could have gone back in time to let Gutenberg know that his invention would lead to such things as *The Bridges of Madison County*, *Dianetics*, and a magazine called *Family Circle*, perhaps he would never have gone through with it.

GYNECOLOGIST: 1. A person who uses the word *speculum* an average of 3,549 more times per year than anyone else. 2. A person who can be cold and dispassionate about exposure to the female reproductive system; very similar to anyone who has been in the same relationship for more than ten years, or a Lutheran.

HABERDASHER: A seller of men's clothing and/or small sewing notions; used only by people who still call carbonated beverages "phosphates" and who still think *gay* means carefree.

HACKER:

THE REASON THAT WHENEVER YOU HIT "RETURN" THESE DAYS, IT OPENS A NEW WINDOW FEATURING A 1953 HOME MOVIE OF NUDISTS PLAYING BADMINTON.

HAGGARD: Gaunt and rough; worn down by life; wasted. A condition commonly seen in barflies, the homeless, and new parents.

HAIRCUT: Something a man would notice his girlfriend had gotten only if she came home bald.

HAIRDRESSER: A person whom you must indulge conversationally no matter how insipid or banal his or her banter may be, remembering that he or she can, at the slightest provocation, make you look like a total dweeb for the next few months.

HALLMARK: A company that has made untold millions off the fact that it's a bitch to come up with something nice to say about the people you love.

The Official Dictionary of Sarcasm

HAMMERED:

ONE OF THE MORE INTERESTING SLANG TERMS FOR BEING INTOXICATED, *HAMMERED* BRINGS WITH IT AN UNSPOKEN IMPLICATION THAT THE OVERINDULGENCE IN ALCOHOL WAS ACTUALLY SOME KIND OF AN ACHIEVEMENT (*"I GOT TOTALLY HAMMERED!"*). THIS PRIDEFUL REFERENCE TO INEBRIATION IS THUS DISTINCT FROM THE FEELINGS ASSOCIATED WITH OTHER DRUNKEN STATES, SUCH AS "BLOTTO" (A KIND OF GOOFY EMBARRASSMENT), "BLITZED" (ALMOST BLIND), "LOADED" (WOBBLY AND INCOHERENT), "PLASTERED" (STIFF AND IMMOVABLE), OR "THREE SHEETS TO THE WIND" (BLISSFULLY UNAWARE THAT YOU ARE DOZING OFF ON THE SHOULDER OF A THREE-HUNDRED-POUND BIKER).

HANDKERCHIEF:
A FASHION ACCESSORY FOR THOSE WHO ENJOY WALKING AROUND WITH THEIR OWN CRUSTY, DRIED SNOT IN THEIR BREAST POCKET.

HAPPY: What we remember being when we were young at those times when we cannot stand how much things suck right now. Experienced with the tacit understanding that it probably sucked back then, too.

HAPPY-GO-LUCKY: Mentally unstable; a person who goes through life experiencing joy for no apparent reason, thus giving the appearance of being someone with whom there is something terribly wrong.

HARASSMENT: Unwanted attention or torment—often concerning inappropriate sexual conduct in the work-place. Such behavior is ill advised, as it causes stress and hardship; however, those who indulge in it soon realize that the resulting legal fees will metaphorically deprive them of the part of their body that caused them to act like such jerks in the first place.

HARD COPY: A prinout for your records of a document created on a computer, which pretty much nails the coffin shut on how those freaking things were supposed to cut down on using paper.

HARD DRIVE: The place where your visits to www.jiggles. net are stored.

HARD WORKING: Conscientious behavior of the kind usually exhibited by a sap who doesn't understand that no one is going to thank him for it.

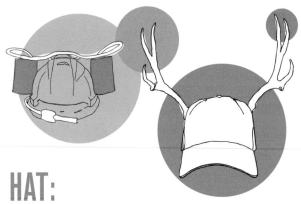

HAT:
A SIMPLE PROTECTIVE HEAD COVERING THAT GOD NEVER MEANT TO FEATURE MOUSE EARS, ANTLERS, OR AN OPPORTUNITY TO DRINK TWO BEERS SIMULTANEOUSLY FROM A SINGLE PLASTIC HOSE.

HATE: A strong, intense dislike or feeling of animosity. Hate is therefore the opposite of love, although if you are patient, you'll get to the hate eventually.

HDTV: A device that allows you to watch crap in greater, more pristine detail.

HEADSTRONG: A quality that we admire in a successful businessperson and a quality we will do anything within our power to crush in a teenager.

HEALTH: A type of insurance plan that covers everything but the rare condition you managed to come down with.

HEALTH FOOD:
SOMETHING A MAN WILL SUCK IT UP FOR AND CLAIM TO ACTUALLY ENJOY IF IT WILL GIVE HIM A SHOT AT ONE OF THOSE COUGAR MOMS AT WHOLE FOODS.

HEALTHY:

WHAT SOMEONE EATING A BACON DOUBLE CHEESEBURGER CALLS SOMEONE WHO IS HAVING A SALAD, SOMEHOW MAKING IT SOUND LIKE THE PERSON WITH THE SALAD IS THE ONE MAKING THE MISTAKE.

HEART: 1. The part of the body that is usually said to have been in the right place when an idiot does something stupid. 2. Female rock band of the 1970s that has been responsible for more alone-in-the-car, head-banging, grip-the-steering-wheel sing-alongs than mom or dad care to admit.

HEARTBROKEN: A state of overwhelming sadness; most commonly experienced by adolescents who do not yet have the emotional distance to grasp just how many more times they are going to get screwed over like this by the time they are twenty-five.

HEART-TO-HEART: An intimate, one-on-one conversation usually initiated by someone who wants to rip you a new one and then say how glad they are that "we" had this little talk.

HEFNER, HUGH:
FOUNDER AND PUBLISHER OF *PLAYBOY* MAGAZINE. A MAN WHO HAS SPENT HIS ENTIRE ADULT LIFE WEARING A SILK BATHROBE AND HANGING OUT IN GROTTOS WITH PHALANXES OF COSMETICALLY-ALTERED FEMALES. THIS IS EITHER DISGRACEFUL OR A DREAM COME TRUE, DEPENDING ON WHOM YOU ARE WITH.

HEMINGWAY, ERNEST: The world's first and only recipient of the Nobel prize for literature who could legitimately be described as *burly*.

HENRY VIII: Sixteenth-century king of England. Noted for his six wives, two of whom he had beheaded. Scholars believe this guy was the first person in history to be referred to as a "piece of work."

HI-LITER: An office supply that is used by morons who have forgotten how to underline.

HIPPIE: Someone God always turns into a corporate executive just to make sure we never lose our sense of irony.

HISTORY: A cumulative account of the ways a bunch of dead people have screwed up in exactly the same ways we are screwing up right now.

HISTORY CHANNEL: A cable television network devoted entirely to stock footage of Adolph Hitler.

HITCHCOCK, SIR ALFRED:

LEGENDARY FILM DIRECTOR. AN OVERWEIGHT, NOT VERY ATTRACTIVE MAN WHO SUBJECTED BEAUTIFUL WOMEN WHOM HE COULD NEVER HAVE TO GRUELING ORDEALS OF TERROR, ALL FOR OUR ENJOYMENT.

The Official Dictionary of Sarcasm

HITLER, ADOLPH: Perhaps the world's biggest butthole, whose prudent decision to blow his own brains out ensured there would be no intellectual-property ownership issues around the hundreds of hours of stock footage of him needed to keep the History Channel in business.

HOBBY: A pleasurable activity calculated to remind you that the things you really love to do don't pay crap.

HOCKEY:
ATTEMPTED MURDER ON ICE.

HOCKEY PUCK: Dolt, stupid. *"You are as stupid as a hockey puck."* Insult created by sarcasm's reigning God, Don Rickles. If you have a problem with this, you are obviously a hockey puck.

HOLIDAY: Any of a series of joyous commemorative dates on which everyone is expected to feel wonderful, making a lot of people who do not happen to feel that way very anxious and ready to haul off and belt the next person who tells them to have a happy one.

HOLLYWOOD: A place where young people with big dreams arrive by the millions each year, then end up living in the gutter, selling their bodies, or going hungry—while only a few truly pitiable, unfortunate idiots end up working in show business.

HOMER: Epic poet of ancient Greece; the man who gave us *The Odyssey*, a tale that has truly had an amazing influence on your eleventh-grade English teacher, although you never actually got around to reading it.

HOMOPHOBIA: A condition that crops up in men when they finally meet the one guy they would turn for.

HOOVER, J. EDGAR: Former FBI head. Noted for ordering an ongoing series of wiretaps on public figures whom he considered "subversive," to which he would listen while wearing a delightful metallic taffeta cocktail dress, white Ferragamo low-heeled pumps, and a charming felt zip-around clutch bearing a distinctive giraffe-print design.

HOPEFULLY: A word meaning "probably not." *"Hopefully, I will be able to make your newborn's upcoming circumcision."*

HORSE WHISPERER:

A PERSON WHO CAN CALM OR TAME A HORSE THROUGH A SERIES OF HUSHED, INTIMATE UTTERANCES AND GENTLE, TENDER FINGER STROKES. IT IS DIFFICULT TO WATCH THIS REMARKABLE TECHNIQUE IN ACTION WITHOUT THINKING, "GET A ROOM."

HOSPITAL: 1. A place of healing in which you are never far from bins clearly marked as toxic waste. 2. An institution where the world's top surgeons stand at the ready to perform a total wallet-ectomy. 3. A depressing building in which the screams of the wounded and infirm blend with the smells of bedpans and antiseptic, yet it is the only place left in the world that still serves those little paper tubs of ice cream with the tiny wooden spoons that you remember as a kid.

HOT: 1. What fast food companies need to tell us our coffee is so that we won't sue them when it spills onto our crotch while we are multitasking on the highway. 2. A sexually appealing person. *"She is so hot."* Usually uttered by someone who hasn't the slightest chance of partaking in the hotness.

HOT DOG:
THE TOENAILS, LIPS, AND EYEBROWS OF VARIOUS ANIMALS SERVED ON A BUN.

HOTEL: A building often used for sexual trysts owing to its incredibly erotic wall art and bedspread selections.

HOUSE: A dwelling that former renters decide to purchase when they can no longer abide their backed-up toilets, burst water pipes, and termites being someone else's problem.

HUMAN: Any of a species of hominids that insist on using the highways, grocery stores, banks, and post offices at the same freaking time as you.

HUMAN RESOURCES: The department within your company that makes sure everybody drinks the Kool-Aid.

HUMMER:

AN OVERSIZED MILITARY VEHICLE THAT HAS BEEN USURPED BY A GENERATION OF YUPPIES, WHOSE ONLY CONTACT WITH ACTION IN THE DESERT IS WHEN THEY PACK UP THEIR REI DESIGNER CAMPING EQUIPMENT AND DRIVE OUT TO JOSHUA TREE TO DROP MUSHROOMS WITH THEIR GOLDEN RETRIEVER.

HUNGOVER: A condition that makes figuring out who was next to you in bed this morning take anywhere from five minutes to a lifetime.

HUNTING: A sport that satisfies men's innate desire to wear earflaps and a tartan jacket while freezing their testicles off by remaining largely motionless for several hours so that every so often they may get the chance to kill something.

HUSBAND:
A MAN WHOSE BEST YEARS ARE BEHIND HIM.

THE PAST

ENTER HERE

HYDRATE:

A WORD USED BY PRETENTIOUS PSEUDOJOCKS—OFTEN THE TYPES WHO DO NOTHING MORE THAN RUN ON A TREADMILL TWICE A WEEK AND FANCY THEMSELVES TRIATHLETES—TO INDICATE WHAT THE REST OF US CALL "DRINKING WATER."

I: The self. It has been the primary factor in every decision made since 1946, resulting not only in the relatively benign consequences of the destruction of community and the dissolving of the family unit but also in the truly heinous and unforgivable development known as reality television.

ICE CREAM:
A CREAMY AND DELECTABLE SLAP IN THE FACE TO THE LACTOSE INTOLERANT.

IDEALIST: A person who foolishly believes you are above screwing him or her over.

IDIOT: See *idealist*.

IDOL: 1. A graven image or effigy of a revered figure. Exemplified by a golden statue of the Buddha, the Lincoln Memorial, or those statues of the Hamburglar outside McDonald's. 2. A person who is the recipient of admiration from another, usually owing to some status in the fields of sports or entertainment. In most cases, idols are dealt with through their publicist, and the admirers' only chance of ever meeting them is to develop a life-threatening illness and hope that they can squeeze out an awkward sympathy bedside visit from an insulated phony who claims to be emotionally invested in their impending death.

IF: A word that is traditionally placed between the phrases "I would sleep with you" and "you had anything remotely interesting to offer."

IKEA:

A RETAIL FURNITURE WAREHOUSE WHOSE MOTTO IS "HERE, *YOU* FREAKIN' BUILD IT."

IMPETUOUS: Acting rashly or hastily. *"Gosh, Ted, your decision to leave your wife and family for that Thai bar girl you met on a Bangkok sex tour sure was impetuous!"*

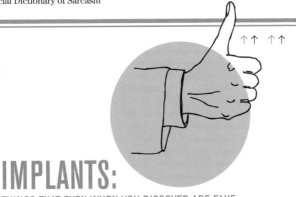

IMPLANTS:
THINGS THAT EVEN WHEN YOU DISCOVER ARE FAKE, SOMEHOW DOESN'T REALLY MATTER.

IMPOTENCE: A condition so frightening and demoralizing to men that when they finally developed a pill to fix it, they made sure it would be good for at least four hours.

INBOX: A place to store things you have no intention of ever dealing with.

INCOHERENT: What you claim your girlfriend is being when you are not yet ready to admit that she is right.

INCOME: Money that your employer should just hand over to your creditors, thereby cutting out the middle man.

INCOMPETENT: A word used to describe the designer of your PC.

INDICTMENT: Something that has been handed down every twenty minutes on Wall Street since roughly 1986.

INJURY: A trauma or wound inflicted upon one's body or one's psyche. While the former can lead to some debilitating medical expenses, there is unfortunately no coverage in place for the damage done by somebody calling you a worthless sack of crap.

INJUSTICE: A WRONG CHARACTERIZED BY A LACK OF FAIRNESS OR EQUITY. FOR EXAMPLE, THE FACT THAT A PERSON NAMED KEVIN FEDERLINE WAS EVER FAMOUS EVEN FOR ONE SINGLE DAY IS AN INJUSTICE OF THE HIGHEST ORDER.

IN-LAW: A person who has the right to tell you how to live your life conferred upon him or her by marriage.

INSIDE SALES:
BUSINESS TRANSACTED WITHOUT LEAVING AN OFFICE, USUALLY VIA THE TELEPHONE. A JOB THAT ALLOWS UNLIMITED OPPORTUNITIES TO MIME A FINGER-DOWN-THE-THROAT GAGGING MOTION IN THE MIDDLE OF A BUSINESS TRANSACTION.

INSURANCE: One of the more audacious scams ever perpetrated upon the general public. Insurance involves a third party who has persuaded people to live in mortal terror of something bad happening and to pay out exorbitant sums of money in the full understanding that it probably won't happen anyway. This creates the illusion of security in the insured, when the fact is that if something really bad did happen, they will still be up the creek six ways from Sunday.

INTELLECTUAL:

SOMEBODY WHO ACTUALLY THINKS ABOUT STUFF. THESE DANGEROUS SUBVERSIVES ARE NOTORIOUSLY GOOD AT BLENDING INTO NORMAL SOCIETY, BUT AS A GENERAL RULE IF THE PERSON NEXT TO YOU WEARS GLASSES AND HAS NEVER SLIPPED A FIVE-DOLLAR TIP INTO A POLE DANCER'S G-STRING, CALL YOUR LOCAL AUTHORITIES IMMEDIATELY.

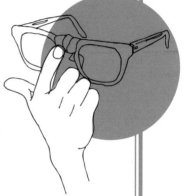

INTENSE: What you insisted on using as a compliment to describe that one creepy guy you dated, until that day they found all those bodies in his crawlspace.

INTERESTING: A word meaning "I have no idea what the hell I'm supposed to say."

INTIMIDATING: Using fear to browbeat or coerce. A tactic often employed by Marine boot camp drill instructors, Mafia enforcers, and people trying to sell you a quality pre-owned Kia.

IPOD: A headphone-assisted device used to help people not be aware of anything, especially that they have wandered into oncoming traffic.

IRS: Internal Revenue Service. A government agency that collects money from its citizens, mostly to fund research into creating the perfect cyborg soldier or to finance a ten-year study on whether we can predict the weather by tracking the ever-changing moods of a fruit fly.

ISP: Internet service provider. A company that gives you access to the magical world of the Internet and all they ask in return is that you endure a home page full of pointless updates on the lives of celebrities, mundane puff pieces on office etiquette, and an unceasing array of animated banner ads, most of which feature dancing shadow people.

IT: Information technology. The department at your workplace that is staffed by every nerd you ever picked on in high school, and whom, ironically, you now depend upon for your very life.

ITUNES:

LIKE A RECORD STORE THAT YOU CAN SHOP IN ONLINE,
EXCEPT YOU PROBABLY DON'T REMEMBER RECORD STORES
ANYWAY.

JACKSON, MICHAEL:

AN INSPIRING, COMPLETELY NORMAL, AND WELL-ADJUSTED
PERSON WHO HAD CLEARLY NOT BEEN AT ALL SCARRED BY
THE RIGORS OF THE ENTERTAINMENT INDUSTRY.

JADED: Older than twenty-two years of age.

JAIL:

1. A PLACE TO EXPERIENCE THE LEAST PRIVACY YOU WILL EVER HAVE WHEN USING A TOILET. 2. ONE'S JOB. 3. ONE'S MARRIAGE. 4. ONE'S SCHOOL. 5. INSERT YOUR PERSONAL HELL HERE.

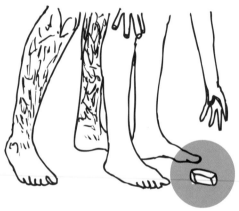

JAZZED: A position on the excitement meter somewhere between "would rather be having oral surgery" and "I just got Dish Network."

JEANS: A style of denim pant originally created for plantation laborers, gold rush miners, and cowboys, all of whom would turn in their freaking graves to think that a bunch of pansies now offer their resilient work clothes in boot cut, flare cut, acid washed, stone washed, prewashed, tapered leg, and, God help us, "relaxed fit," whatever the hell that means.

JELL-O:

1. A GELATIN DESSERT ITEM FOR THOSE WHO PREFER THEIR SUGAR TO BE GREEN AND TO WIGGLE. 2. WHEN PREPARED WITH VODKA, IT PROVIDES YET ANOTHER WAY FOR A FAMILY-ORIENTED BRAND TO BE ASSOCIATED WITH DRUNKEN YOUNG ADULTS CONSUMING ALCOHOL OFF OF EACH OTHER'S EXPOSED MIDRIFFS.

JEOPARDY!: The television quiz show you have to pretend you suck at if you want to retain credibility with your less intelligent friends.

JERK: What you probably shouldn't have called that cop.

JILTED: Unlike other more benign words for unceremonious rejection such as *dropped*, *spurned*, or *dumped*, *jilted* carries with it the tacit implication that one can expect significant retaliation, usually of the kind involving a butcher-block knife and the unceremonious removal of a certain dangling appendage.

JOB: Your punishment for never winning the lottery.

JOE SIX-PACK:

A GENERIC TERM FOR THE AVERAGE CITIZEN, YET ITS IMAGE OF A BEER-BELLIED, BRAIN-DEAD SLOTH LYING GELATINOUSLY ON A SAGGING COUCH WITH HIS PANTS OPEN AND GUZZLING HALF A DOZEN OLD MILWAUKEES BETWEEN EXPLOSIVE BELCHES HAS SOMEHOW ATTAINED A NEGATIVE CONNOTATION.

JOGGER: Someone who thinks they can forestall death by doing something that looks like it is killing them.

JOHN, ELTON:

LEGENDARY POP STAR WHO HAS DRESSED FAR MORE CONSERVATIVELY SINCE COMING OUT AS A GAY MAN THAN HE EVER DID BEFORE WE KNEW FOR SURE THAT THE SEQUINED BODY STOCKINGS, FEATHER BOAS, AND FOUR HUNDRED DIFFERENT PAIRS OF DAY-GLO GLASSES MIGHT HAVE BEEN TRYING TO TELL US SOMETHING.

JOKE: An amusing anecdote that is more often than not told by someone who is about as funny as an engine block.

JOYCE, JAMES: Famous Irishman who was noted for creating rambling, stream-of-consciousness, and often incomprehensible stories even without the aid of a pub.

JPEG: A digital technology that makes it possible for you to endure the same barrage of boring vacation photos you thought you would never have to sit through again since the day the Internet made it possible for you to cut off all in-person contact with morons.

JUDGE:
THE OTHER PROFESSION IN WHICH SOMEONE WEARING A BLACK ROBE STANDS ON A RAISED PLATFORM AND SEEMS TO ENJOY CONDEMNING PEOPLE.

JUICE: Something children won't drink unless it comes in a tiny square box with its own straw; something adults won't drink unless it costs as much as their mocha latte and has been repackaged by corporate spin to include pomegranate, spirulina, and antioxidants, like anybody knows what antioxidants are anyway.

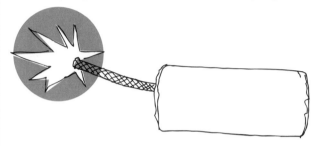

JULY FOURTH:
AN EXCUSE TO GET DRUNK, LIGHT THINGS ON FIRE, AND PERHAPS EVEN LOSE ONE OR MORE OF THE DIGITS ON YOUR HANDS, ALL THE WHILE KNOWING YOU CAN BLAME IT ON LOVING YOUR COUNTRY.

JURY DUTY: Part of the very backbone of a judicial system that sets the United States apart from every other democratic country, this is a proud and honorable civic duty that all Americans should do everything in their power to get out of.

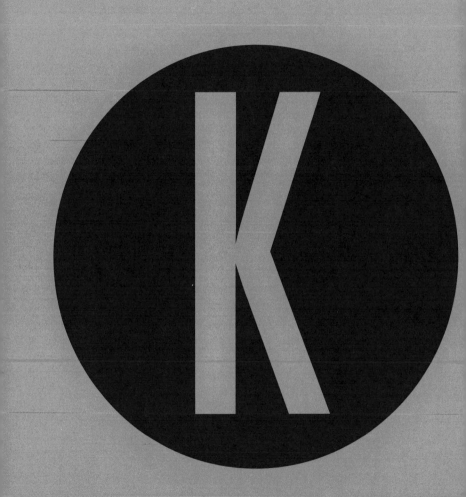

KAFKA, FRANZ: Czech-born author of the early twentieth century whose nightmarish novels feature tormented souls plagued by personal demons and kept in a suffocating state of repression by an uncaring dominant government. "The Feel-Good Writer of The Year!" (*Prague Morning Herald*, 1921).

KARAOKE: A once-in-a-lifetime chance for lonely, untalented people to be even more sad and pitiable than they are in everyday life.

KETCHUP: A vegetable that finally got its due when it was recognized by the Reagan administration in the 1980s.

KEYBOARD:

1. A MUSICAL TOY THAT YOU CHOOSE TO BUY YOUR TODDLER AT YOUR OWN PERIL. 2. IN COMPUTER TERMINOLOGY, THE THING YOU SPEND MOST OF THE TIME POUNDING ON WITH YOUR FIST.

KINDERGARTEN: Former platform for early learning and playtime; currently the time in a child's life when he or she better damn well decide exactly what they want out of life and get going on a plan to make it happen.

The Official Dictionary of Sarcasm

KINKY:

DEVIANT, ESPECIALLY IN ONE'S SEXUALITY. PROBLEM IS, MOST OF THE STUFF THAT IS CONSIDERED KINKY—LIKE LEATHER, WHIPS, CHAINS, AND NIPPLE CLAMPS—IS ACTUALLY FUNNY AS HELL. AND NOTHING KILLS SEXUAL EXCITEMENT LIKE BEING LAUGHED AT FOR LOOKING LIKE A TOTAL JACKASS.

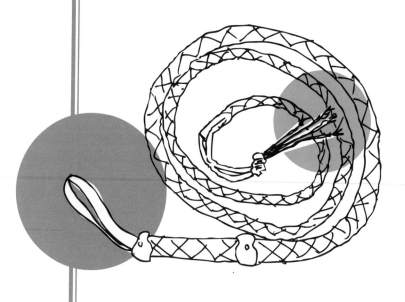

KISS: 1. The touch of another's lips as an expression of affection. Only a few generations ago, a kiss was considered a risqué and even dangerous introduction to physical intimacy. Nowadays, it is usually bypassed completely in favor of an immediate teen pregnancy. 2. A 1970s glitter rock band featuring men in elaborate make-up and black spandex that gave a generation of antisocial cretins permission to rock out.

KNOWLEDGE: Wisdom gained through study or experience. Knowledge comes in handy during one's school years, when one can use it to puke back a bunch of facts on multiple-choice tests to get through the ordeal known as one's education. Knowledge is then completely ignored during one's adulthood, as courtship, marriage, and family consume the mind. Finally, in one's golden years, one can share all the accumulated knowledge of a lifetime with a bunch of ungrateful young people who assume you are senile and who pay little attention. Incidentally, many of these young people may well be your coworkers at the McDonald's at which you were forced to work to generate the retirement income you need to supplement your rapidly dwindling Social Security.

KOSHER: 1. Food that conforms to Jewish nutritional laws, which were handed down by God in order that the Chosen People would never experience flavor. 2. Also used as a generic term to imply legitimacy. *"I know most people don't sell stereo equipment out of the back of a panel van, but don't worry, it's strictly kosher."*

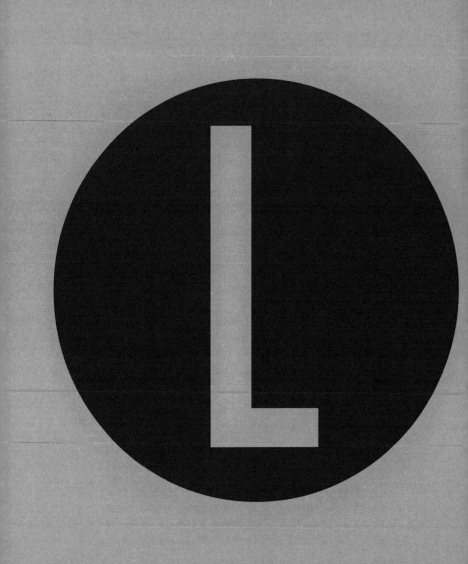

LANDFILL: A sanitized, polite term for a place that used to be called "the dump." Unfortunately, that term only reminded people of the thing they were metaphorically *taking* on the earth every time they blithely tossed all their refuse onto an ever-burgeoning mound of dirt and solid waste.

LANDLORD: The only person you cannot stand who nonetheless has keys to your place.

LAPTOP:

A PRODUCT CREATED OUT OF THE INCREASING DEMAND FOR A CONTAINER FULL OF POTENTIALLY TOXIC COMPUTER PARTS TO BE POSITIONED ABOVE ONE'S GENITALS.

LAS VEGAS:

A NEVADA GAMBLING AND ENTERTAINMENT MECCA THAT SELLS ITSELF AS A NAUGHTY DESTINATION FOR THE SEXUALLY ADVENTUROUS NIGHTCLUB SET, WHEN IN REALITY IT CONTAINS MOSTLY DOUGHY FAMILIES FROM THE MIDWEST WHOSE IDEA OF A NIGHT AT THE THEATER INVOLVES EITHER A LIGHT SHOW OR A MAGICIAN AND ROW UPON ROW OF INFIRM EMPHYSEMA CASES GOING FROM ONE PENNY SLOT MACHINE TO ANOTHER ON THEIR MOBILITY SCOOTERS. SEXY STUFF, INDEED.

LAUNDROMAT: A place in which you may well meet the man or woman of your dreams, if only because it's bound to happen when everything you own is in a giant top loader and you're wearing a perspiration-stained twenty-year-old Sammy Hagar "I Can't Drive 55" tour T-shirt and mustard-stained sweats over a pair of yellowed, crusty underwear.

LAWYER: A job in which 97 percent of those practicing it somehow manage to give the entire profession a bad name.

LEAF BLOWER:
A DEVICE THAT ANSWERS THE AGE-OLD SCIENTIFIC QUESTION, HEY, CAN WE DESIGN A RAKE THAT MAKES NOISE?

LEATHER: A type of material that when worn as a jacket leaves even the most badass biker only a heartbeat away from being a member of the Village People.

LED ZEPPELIN:

INFLUENTIAL BRITISH BAND FORMED IN THE 1960S THAT INTRODUCED THE WORLD TO BLUES-INFLUENCED HEAVY METAL, FOLK-INSPIRED ROCK, AND CUCUMBERS DOWN THE TROUSERS.

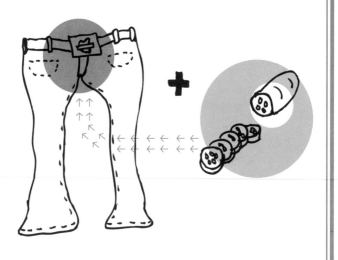

LEFT: 1. A sociopolitical stance that leans toward the liberal, often adopted by movie stars who make so much money that they will never have to mix with the proletariat scum they claim to champion. 2. A turn signal that remains in a constant ON position in cars driven by anyone over sixty-five.

LENIN, VLADIMIR:

EARLY-TWENTIETH-CENTURY RUSSIAN BOLSHEVIK REVOLUTIONARY. AS WITH MANY POLITICAL IDEALISTS, HIS REIGN BEGAN WITH GOOD INTENTIONS BUT CONTAINED SUSTAINED PERIODS OF MADNESS AND BLOODSHED—MUCH LIKE YOUR HIGH SCHOOL VALEDICTORIAN'S HORRENDOUS BOTCHING OF THE STUDENT COUNCIL PRESIDENCY SEAT.

LESBIAN: A woman who has finally figured out that men are largely unnecessary.

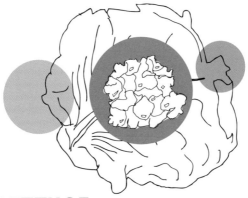

LETTUCE:

A TASTELESS PLANT ONE MUST INCLUDE AS THE BASE PORTION OF ONE'S SALAD BAR VISIT, SOLELY TO MAINTAIN THE ILLUSION THAT ONE IS EATING HEALTHILY EVEN THOUGH ONE'S PLATE WILL SOON BE PILED HIGH WITH THE MAYONNAISE-LADEN MACARONI AND POTATO CONCOCTIONS THAT GOT YOU TO THE SALAD BAR IN THE FIRST PLACE.

LIBERAL: A person who advocates a loose attitude toward certain societal constraints even though he or she will probably burn in Hell for it.

LIBRARIAN: A woman who, much like her counterpart the plain and prim assistant to a movie scientist, magically transforms into a stunning beauty when she takes off her glasses and undoes her ponytail.

LIBRARY: A place for ordinary citizens to reconnect with the homeless and the freaks of the world who still read.

LIE: Something politicians accuse each other of doing in an endless and laughably ironic cycle of the pot calling the kettle black.

LIFEGUARD:
A PERSON TRAINED IN WATER RESCUE WHO NEVER USUALLY HAS ANYTHING TO DO BUT LOOK DOWN FROM AN ELEVATED CHAIR AT A HORDE OF HALF-NAKED FAMILIES WHILE BEING VIGILANT ABOUT APPLYING FRESH GLOBS OF ZINC OXIDE TO THE BRIDGE OF HIS OR HER NOSE. HOWEVER, AS DEPICTED ON THE TELEVISION PROGRAM *BAYWATCH*, LIFEGUARDS ALSO APPARENTLY RUN UP AND DOWN THE BEACH ALL DAY IN SLOW MOTION WHEN THEY ARE NOT FOILING INTERNATIONAL DRUG-SMUGGLING RINGS THAT OPERATE OUT OF INFLATABLE KAYAKS.

LIKE: A word that somewhere in the late twentieth century began to be used as the connective tissue in all spoken sentences, despite the fact that the words on either side of it need nothing to connect them in the first place. Example: the following sentence functions perfectly well without the additional use of the word *like*. *"And he was so, like, unreasonable, and I thought, like, Why are you all up in my face? and then, like, he just walked away."* Hence, we prove that *like* is, like, totally useless.

LINCOLN, ABRAHAM:
SIXTEENTH PRESIDENT OF THE UNITED STATES. BORN IN THE LOG CABIN THAT HE BUILT WITH HIS OWN TWO HANDS.

LINK: Diminutive of *hyperlink*, or the coded element placed in an electronic communication that allows navigation to another Internet location. In 90 percent of e-mails sent by your annoying friends, this link will get you to a viral video about some guy who does incredibly realistic sidewalk paintings or an inspiring story about a polar bear who made friends with a ferret.

LIST: An ordered array of words or subjects compiled into an itemized series. Neither the television network VH-1 nor the news publication *USA Today* could exist without this stylistic convention.

LISTENING: Paying close attention; taking an interest in what is being communicated. A skill that has yet to be developed in men or cats.

LITTLE LEAGUE:

A YOUTH SPORTING EVENT THAT PROVIDES A SOCIALLY ACCEPTABLE WAY FOR ADULTS TO SCAR THEIR CHILDREN WITH THE BURDEN OF THEIR PARENTS' SHATTERED, UNFULFILLED DREAMS.

LOGIC: The principles of reasoned thought. Brazenly abandoned on a daily basis either by your employer, your spouse, or the president of the United States. And, let's be honest, most days it's all three.

LOL: Acronym for *laugh out loud*. Usually employed because the acronym for *that joke you forwarded was not the least bit funny but I have so few friends outside of cyberspace that I am going to humor you by telling you it was so that I can continue this desperate nonfriendship electronically* (TJYFWNTLBFBIHSFFOOCTIAGTHYBTYIWSTICCTDNE) is a bit unwieldy.

LONGFELLOW, HENRY WADSWORTH: Nineteenth-century American poet most famous for *Paul Revere's Ride*, which set its author the challenge of how to make glaring historical inaccuracies rhyme.

LORD OF THE RINGS:

A TRILOGY OF EXTREMELY POPULAR FANTASY BOOKS FEATURING GNOME-LIKE HOBBITS BATTLING EVIL WARLORDS FOR CONTROL OF A MAGICAL PLACE CALLED MIDDLE EARTH. THE SUCCESSFUL SERIES OF FILMS BASED ON THESE BOOKS INTRODUCED AN ENTIRE UNSUSPECTING GENERATION TO SOMETHING THEIR PARENTS UNDERSTOOD ONLY WHEN THEY WERE STONED OUT OF THEIR GOURDS.

LOTTERY, THE: A way for states to raise money for programs like education, in the hopes of one day raising a group of people smart enough to realize they will never win the lottery.

LOVE: A deep and abiding affection that compels you to go to the bitter end with someone you should probably have ditched at the altar.

LOW: 1. Feeling dejected or blue. Should be immediately addressed with medication, so that your friends don't have to put up with you constantly sucking all the energy out of the room. 2. Contemptible; *a low blow*— such as telling someone they have come to resemble their dog.

LOYAL: Unwavering and steadfast in one's allegiance. Usually rewarded with being among the first to be led to the death squads after the coup.

LUCK: An intangible series of factors that lead to a good outcome. By and large, these crazy, unpredictable fortunate circumstances are experienced by people who come from money and connections and not by poor schlubs like you. Go figure.

LUNCH LADY:
THE REASON YOU STILL CANNOT FUNCTION SEXUALLY ON THOSE RARE OCCASIONS WHEN YOU ENCOUNTER A HAIRNET.

LUST: God's way of giving overworked, stressed-out congressmen a convenient way to end the careers they lack the courage to end for themselves.

MAC: 1. A type of computer that confers upon its owner a sense of moral superiority, which is usually combined with a snotty, holier-than-thou attitude toward anyone who continues to use a PC. 2. Major—perhaps the ultimate—comfort food (note: only when combined with *and cheese*).

MACHO:

A FORM OF OVERSTATED MASCULINITY, REQUIRING MALES TO LIVE IN A STATE OF CONSTANT READINESS TO WHIP IT OUT AND SEE WHOSE IS BIGGER.

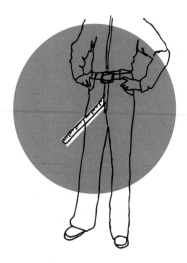

MAGIC: A force that can affect events through supernatural means. It is this force that you remain certain will intercede in your life right up until the point when you have to meet with the debt consolidation company.

MAN: Though it refers to the male of the human species, this word is also a generic term for all of humanity, thereby letting us know which gender to blame when things go down the tubes.

MANAGER:
A PERSON WHOSE AUTHORITY IS OFTEN UNDERMINED BY A PAPER HAT AND A NAME TAG.

MAP: Before the invention of the GPS, this paper representation of a given geographical area was pointedly left unused by hopelessly lost men who were too proud to consult anything but their internal compass for directions. Ironically, those same men now happily take orders from a female voice emitting from their dashboard.

MARCO POLO: Thirteenth- and fourteenth-century Venetian explorer widely assumed to have brought the noodles that became spaghetti back with him from China. But his poor sainted mama would turn in her grave if she knew that her son's pasta is now routinely topped with spaghetti sauce from a jar that is loaded with high-fructose corn syrup.

MARGINALIZED: Forced into obscurity, where you belong.

MARIJUANA:

A DANGEROUS GATEWAY DRUG THAT CAN LEAD TO MORE SERIOUS ADDICTIONS LIKE GUITAR HERO AND DORITOS, AND WORKING RETAIL UNTIL YOU ARE FIFTY.

MARRIAGE: Sucking it up and buying the cow after years of getting the milk for free.

MARSHMALLOW:
A SPONGY CONFECTION THAT IS DELICIOUS ON ITS OWN, WHEN ROASTED OVER AN OPEN FIRE, OR WHEN FORMED INTO THE CREEPY LIKENESS OF A BABY CHICKEN WITH LITTLE DOT MARKS FOR EYES.

MASOCHIST: A person with a job.

MATERIALISM: A belief that gaining more and more possessions will eventually provide one with happiness. Of all personal belief systems, this one is the most fun to try and prove wrong.

The Official Dictionary of Sarcasm

MATERNAL: A beautiful, nurturing term used in online dating profiles to indicate a complete lack of hotness.

MATURITY: A fully grown, evolved state of being; often achieved on the day when you gain satisfaction in putting another's needs before your own. If you are smart enough not to have a kid to force you into this awful predicament, you should be able to coast just fine without it.

MAYONNAISE: The product of a hard-fought quest to invent a product capable of transforming a can of chunk light tuna into something edible.

MEAT:
SOMETHING THAT WHEN COMBINED WITH THE WORD *LOAF* INDICATES THAT THE COOK HAS RUN OUT OF OPTIONS.

MECHANIC: A person who goes through years of training to never hear the same sound coming from your car that you were hearing before you brought it in.

MEDIA: ← ← ← ← ← ←
← ← ← ← ← ←
LIARS WITH ACCESS TO EYE-CATCHING GRAPHICS.

MEDICATION: Your friendly and caring medical professional's way of saying "I'm out of ideas."

MEDIEVAL: Characteristic of the Middle Ages, a time when handsome knights fought battles for fair maidens in the name of chivalry. This pain-in-the-ass time still persists in the public imagination, making it difficult for women not to form unrealistic expectations and making it difficult for guys to skate by with the occasional belch every once in a while.

MEDIOCRITY: The condition of being unremarkable or ordinary. Also known as one's life, except maybe that one semester abroad.

MEETING: A business term meaning "officially sanctioned waste of time."

MENU: 1. A list of food options handed to you at a restaurant so that you may decide to have the same unimaginative thing you always have. 2. A series of number-coded options in an automated phone service menu, each one calculated to plunge you into a labyrinthine nightmare of never reaching a live person and being taken further into the abyss every time you press "pound." 3. The series of three hundred applications your computer screen provides to you, little knowing that you are too frightened to try anything but Word.

METAL: A type of music usually prefixed with the word *heavy* to indicate that each band member's hair weighs more than that person's entire body.

METER MAID: A thankless job whose approval rating hovers steadily somewhere between Britney Spears and Vlad the Impaler.

MICHELANGELO: Italian artist active chiefly in the sixteenth century and best known for his frescoes of the Genesis story on the ceiling of the Sistine Chapel and the nude male statue of David, the latter of which has caused millions of repressed American tourists to try and look as if they are not staring at a perfectly rendered marble penis during their visit to Florence.

MICROMANAGER: A person who had his or her ability to chill out surgically removed at birth.

MICROWAVE: A device for those who prefer a dash of radioactivity in their popcorn.

MIDLIFE: That bittersweet time in the aging process during which you are absolutely convinced that boffing a twenty-eight-year-old makes you twenty-eight again, too.

MILE-HIGH CLUB:
THE ONLY CLUB THAT HAS MANAGED TO RETAIN ITS SEXY CACHET DESPITE THE FACT THAT TO BECOME A MEMBER YOU HAVE TO FORNICATE AMID THE HEADY AROMA OF RECYCLED HUMAN WASTE WHILE TRYING UNSUCCESSFULLY TO AVOID TURNING ON THE MINIATURE WATER FAUCET WITH YOUR BUTT CHEEK.

MIME: A performer whose sole purpose is to annoy the hell out of you and at whom it will do absolutely no good to yell, "Shut up!"

MINIVAN:

A VEHICLE THAT LETS EVERY WOMAN ON THE PLANET KNOW YOU ARE AS OUT OF CIRCULATION AS THEY COME.

MINUTE: An interval of time that seems quite short and inconsequential until you use up 185 of them fruitlessly Googling the current whereabouts of your last three relationships.

MISS: 1. A failure to attain something. *"I'm sorry I missed your party; I had something fun I wanted to do."* 2. To pine or long for. *"Damn, I miss Dutch apple Pop-Tarts."* 3. A term of respect used when addressing a young woman. *"Excuse me, miss, how much for an around-the-world?"*

MONA LISA, THE: Perhaps the world's most famous painting, da Vinci's portrait of an unknown woman with an enigmatic half-grin is such a big load of nothing that you cannot believe you wasted three hours of your visit to Paris just to get within ten yards of it. Plus it's, like, really small. What a rip.

MONDAY: One of fifty-two opportunities we are given each and every year to wake up and question what the hell we are doing with our lives.

MONEY: Something the people whose faces ended up on our currency never had to stress about.

MONKEY:

ANY OF THE VARIOUS MEMBERS OF THE PRIMATE ORDER WHO LIKE NOTHING BETTER THAN TO DRESS UP IN FUNNY OUTFITS AND PLAY TOY INSTRUMENTS FOR THE AMUSEMENT OF HUMANS.

MONOPOLY: A board game that allows family members the thrill of screwing each other over financially.

MOON, THE:
A SATELLITE IN THE SOLAR SYSTEM ABOUT WHICH PEOPLE SEEMED INORDINATELY INTERESTED FOR ABOUT TWENTY MINUTES BACK IN THE 1960S AND HAS SINCE FALLEN OUT OF FAVOR AS A POP-CULTURE PHENOMENON. YOU KNOW MEN: PROBABLY AFTER THEY FINISHED LANDING ON IT, THEY JUST CAST IT ASIDE AND HOPED IT WOULD NEVER CALL.

MORON: Anyone who is not driving as consistently perfectly as you.

MORTGAGE: Heartburn in paper form.

The Official Dictionary of Sarcasm

MOTHER:

1. THE WOMAN WHO ENDURED MANY HOURS OF EXCRUCIATING PAIN TO BRING YOU INTO THE WORLD AND WHOM YOU REPAY FOR THIS SACRIFICE BY STAYING SINGLE AND DRIFTING FROM JOB TO JOB, NOT EVEN CARING THAT WITH EACH FOOLISH MISSTEP YOU MAKE, YOU DRIVE A HOT SABER DEEPER AND DEEPER INTO HER HEART. AND DON'T EVER FORGET THAT SHE LOVES YOU. 2. A SAINT. (ITALIAN AMERICAN MEN ONLY.)

MOTHER THERESA: Someone who spent her entire life caring for the poor and downtrodden just to make you feel like a hardhearted, unfeeling creep.

MOVIE: A form of filmed entertainment for which we continue to shell out significant portions of our hard-earned cash despite the fact that 80 to 90 percent of the product we pay for is appalling, execrable dreck. These are extraordinarily bad odds, which we would never continue to play on any of the other goods and services we consume, not to mention that the actors we are supporting with our money are all much richer than we are. Someday, someone will get hip to this collective cultural insanity and stop the madness. On the other hand, maybe it's all worth it just to see some nudity every once in a while.

MOVIE CRITIC:
A PERSON WHO HAS DUPED HIS OR HER EMPLOYER INTO PAYING HIM OR HER TO PUBLISH THINGS THAT NOBODY EVER READS.

MOVIE THEATER: A place where one can sit in comfort and view the latest motion-picture entertainment surrounded by a bunch of other people who seem to think they are at a WWF Smackdown.

The Official Dictionary of Sarcasm

MOZART, WOLFGANG AMADEUS:

EIGHTEENTH-CENTURY CLASSICAL COMPOSER WHO BEGAN CRAFTING WORKS OF MUSICAL GENIUS AT AGE FIVE. AND STILL THE SUCKER NEVER WON A GRAMMY.

MRS.: The proper way to address a married woman when you are around people who do not know you are having her on the side.

MULTITASKING: Something your friends try to deny they are doing while talking to you on the phone, even though you keep hearing the prerecorded phrase, "You've got mail" in the background of your entire conversation.

MUSICIAN: A person who is genetically incapable of feeling shame or guilt over being supported by his girlfriend.

MYSPACE: An Internet site where jobless folk who are incapable of feeling shame or guilt over being supported by their girlfriends can post the crappy MP3s they spent all day recording on Garage Band.

NANNY:

A YOUNG WOMAN WHO RAISES AND NURTURES THE CHILDREN OF THOSE WHO HAVE BETTER THINGS TO DO THAN DEVELOP EMOTIONAL TIES TO THEIR OFFSPRING.

NAKED: Lacking clothing or outward covering; as such, one can be physically naked or emotionally naked. The trick is to not be the latter while you are the former unless you are prepared to cry during sex.

NAPOLEON:

NINETEENTH-CENTURY EMPEROR OF FRANCE, FAMOUSLY DEPICTED WITH HIS HAND INSIDE HIS SHIRT. DON'T ASK—IT'S A FRENCH THING.

NARCISSIST: Someone who is totally and excessively preoccupied with themselves. Derived from Narcissus, the Greek mythological character who fell in love with his own reflection. So, in contemporary terms, if you catch anyone trying to dry hump the mirror, it's fair to say you've got yourself a narcissist.

NARROW-MINDED: Anyone who cannot get past your polygamy.

NATURAL: A buzzword that exploded in the 1960s and still regularly appears on food packaging today. Of course, the definition of the term has broadened considerably since its inception and now basically refers to any food product that does not contain plutonium.

NEIGHBOR:
A USUALLY INCONSIDERATE, LOUD, AND ALL-AROUND HATEFUL PERSON WHOM YOU ONLY REFRAIN FROM ASSAULTING PHYSICALLY BECAUSE HE HAS NOT YET RETURNED YOUR CORDLESS DRILL.

NETFLIX: A convenient Internet-based delivery system for movie rentals that effectively killed your local mom-and-pop video store, leaving mom and pop to lose everything they had, live in the street, and eventually die from sleeping too near the runoff from the sewer drain by the bridge over the interstate. I hope you're happy, Netflix.

NETIQUETTE:

A SET OF IMPLIED RULES USED TO FACILITATE COURTEOUS COMMUNICATION IN CYBERSPACE. CHIEF AMONG THESE IS THE UNSPOKEN AGREEMENT TO NOT TYPE IN ALL UPPERCASE LETTERS, AS THIS CAN GIVE THE READER THE IMPRESSION THAT YOU ARE SHOUTING. AND GOD KNOWS YOU WOULD NOT WANT ANYONE TO THINK YOU ARE SHOUTING WHEN YOU TYPE "TAKE ME OFF YOUR *!!%#*(@)^** MAILING LIST, YOU SPAM-HAPPY FREAK."

NEUROTIC: A term from the field of psychology meaning "gradually disinvited from all social events, especially ones at restaurants."

NEVER: In no instance; not ever. *Never* is a word used to declare that we have limitations regarding the doing of undesirable or humiliating things. It is usually invoked most vehemently about two weeks before financial hardship forces us to suck it up and do them.

NEVERLAND:

A RANCH OWNED BY MICHAEL JACKSON THAT FEATURES A VERY SPECIAL PETTING ZOO, AS WELL AS AN AREA WHERE ONE CAN PLAY WITH ANIMALS.

NEW AGE:

ANY OF THE CLASS OF HUMANS WHO BELIEVE THEY CAN ATTAIN HIGHER CONSCIOUSNESS BY WEARING DRAWSTRING PANTS, REFUSING TO BATHE, AND EATING MUESLI.

NEWS:

WAR, MURDER, NATURAL DISASTERS, AND A FAILING ECONOMY SERVED IN CONVENIENT, EASY-TO-FORGET TWO-MINUTE INCREMENTS AND TOPPED OFF WITH AN INSPIRING STORY OF COURAGE ABOUT EITHER AN ORANGUTAN OR SOMEBODY WITH A TUMOR.

NEWS, LOCAL: Everything contained in the previous entry, plus sports, weather, and some really unforgivable hair.

NEWSPAPER:
THE EIGHT-TRACK TAPE OF THE INFORMATION AGE.

NEWTON, SIR ISAAC: English astronomer and physicist active in the seventeenth and eighteenth centuries. He developed the theory that the universe is governed by the same gravitational pull as earth by submitting to the repeated humiliation of being hit by a piece of fruit.

NEXT: A word that can sometimes take hours, maybe even days, to be uttered by a clerk at the Department of Motor Vehicles.

NIAGARA FALLS: The only thing that is just as big, loud, and in-your-face in Canada as it is in the United States.

NICHOLSON, JACK: Iconic American film actor noted for playing the kind of volatile, rowdy, uncaring user-psychopath that women find irresistible.

NIETZSCHE, FRIEDRICH:

NIHILISTIC GERMAN PHILOSOPHER OF THE NINETEENTH CENTURY WHO POSITED THAT GOD WAS DEAD, THEREBY GIVING EVERY TURTLENECK-WEARING HIPSTER A REASON TO SIT IN THE CORNER OF THE COFFEEHOUSE LOOKING INTENSE AND JUST WAITING FOR SOMEONE TO GET HIM GOING ON WHY LIFE IS ULTIMATELY MEANINGLESS.

NIPPLE: A perfectly innocuous protrusion on the chest of the human body that even when fully exposed on a man and seen by a woman produces little or no discernible response, yet that same protrusion when barely glimpsed on a woman by a man never fails to inspire whiplash and a thin stream of Pavlovian drool.

NITPICK: To rip someone a new one without leaving anything out.

NIXON, RICHARD:

THIRTY-SEVENTH PRESIDENT OF THE UNITED STATES, WHO MUST HAVE BEEN A REAL DOOZY OR OLIVER STONE WOULD NEVER HAVE MADE A FILM ABOUT HIM.

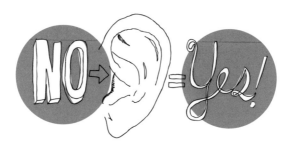

NO:
A WORD NOT UNDERSTOOD BY DOGS, CHILDREN, OR COMMISSIONED SALESPEOPLE.

NON-PROFIT: A business that is plagued by as much infighting, inefficiency, and politics as any other, except all the employees wear Birkenstocks and clothing made of hemp.

NOSTALGIA: A longing for events in the past. Nostalgia is an inexplicable, irrational force, so capable of convincing us that everything was much better decades ago that we actually proclaim, with a straight face, that Wang Chung and *Batteries Not Included* were artistic efforts of Real Genius. Which, by the way, was another awesome movie. Dude, Val Kilmer knocked that one out of the park.

NOVEL: A bogus term of respect bestowed upon a book that keeps interrupting all the good sex and violence with detailed descriptions of the how the wind stirred the branches of the damned trees.

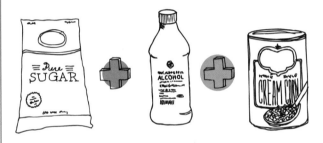

NUCLEAR WEAPON:

A DEVICE THAT IS NOW IN THE HANDS OF JUST ABOUT EVERYONE AND CAN APPARENTLY BE ASSEMBLED WITH LITTLE MORE THAN CONFECTIONERS' SUGAR, ISOPROPYL ALCOHOL, AND A CAN OF CREAMED CORN.

NUN: A woman whose decision to marry God has left her more than willing to open up a can of whoop-ass on you at the slightest provocation.

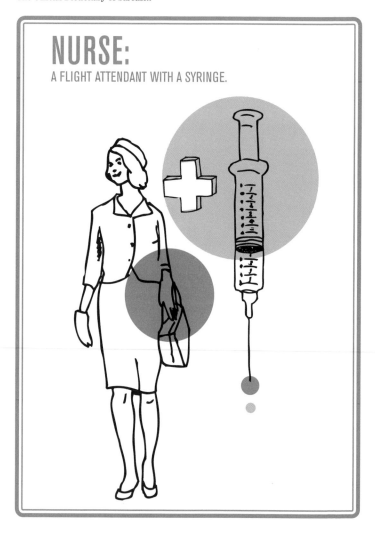

NURSE:
A FLIGHT ATTENDANT WITH A SYRINGE.

OBLIGATION:

A FEELING OF BEING MORALLY IN DEBT TO PEOPLE TO THE POINT OF BEING BOUND TO INTERACT WITH THEM SOCIALLY. THIS IS THE KIND OF EMOTIONALLY DRAINING FEELING THAT MAKES YOU WISH THE PERSON WHO PULLED YOU FROM THE RAGING RIVER AND SNATCHED YOU FROM THE JAWS OF DEATH WASN'T SUCH A FLAMING BUTTHOLE.

OBLIVIOUS: Unaware, not cognizant. Rather like the way teenagers, debutantes, and fish go through life.

OBSCENE: A word whose definition is usually given by a group of creepy old judges in loose-fitting robes who sit around behind closed doors watching pornography all day to decide if they find it morally objectionable.

OFFENSIVE: Repugnant or unpleasant to one's personal tastes. There is no way to gauge when anything one says or does may prove to be offensive, so telling jokes about how the members of certain ethnic or religious groups are really stupid is something you should only do when you are around other racists.

OFFICE:

1. THE PLACE WHERE ALL THE SOUL-SUCKING FAERIES LIVE.
2. THE LAST LOCATION ON EARTH WHERE THERE IS ALWAYS AT LEAST ONE PERSON WHO IS STILL INTO GARFIELD.

Soul

OFFLINE: A frightening state of near-death panic in which someone makes the foolish decision to log off the Internet, despite knowing that it will deprive them of the unabated access to an endless barrage of useless information, which was the only thing letting them know they were alive in the first place.

OFF THE HOOK: Far exceeding expectations of being totally dope and fresh. If this expression is not already so yesterday by the time you read this, then it most definitely will be within the year.

OIL:
1. THE MAIN REASON MANY RECENT WARS HAVE BEEN FOUGHT. 2. THE MAIN REASON MANY ZITS HAVE TO BE POPPED. 3. THE MAIN REASON FOR OLIVES.

OLD: What people feel like when their references to leisure suits and Three Dog Night are met with blank stares.

OLD-FASHIONED: A word used to describe either a cocktail made out of whiskey and bitters or someone who believes in waiting at least a week to consummate the relationship.

OLIVE GARDEN:
THE ONLY AUTHENTIC ITALIAN DINING ESTABLISHMENT WHEREIN YOU PAY SOMEONE TO MICROWAVE A FROZEN DINNER FOR YOU.

The Official Dictionary of Sarcasm

OMG: An acronym that could actually *be* the phrase it is meant to indicate by simply adding all of four damn letters.

ON CALL:
A TERM YOUR JOB USES TO INDICATE THE LESS FORMAL NOTION OF "YOU MY BEEYOTCH."

ONLINE: Participating in the mass hallucination that millions of losers each sitting alone in front of their own tiny screen is an example of how the Internet brings people together.

ON-RAMP: A section of road on which a huge percentage of morons repeatedly think that going twenty miles per hour is the perfect strategy for merging into six lanes of maniacs doing seventy or better.

OPINIONATED: Knowing absolutely nothing really loudly.

OPTIMIST: One who sees the glass half full, even when it is half full of urine.

OPTOMETRIST:

A PERSON WHO GETS THEIR JOLLIES BY FLIPPING BETWEEN TWO DIFFERENT DIOPTERS WHILE ASKING YOU WHICH ONE HELPS YOU TO SEE THE LETTER *E* BETTER, EVEN THOUGH THEY KNOW PERFECTLY WELL THAT THE LETTERS ARE BOTH EXACTLY THE SAME.

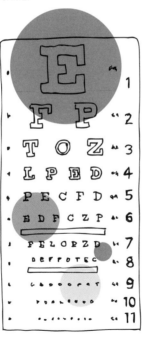

ORAL SEX: Something men think women do because they like it; something women wish men would do even though they hate it.

ORGANIC: Mistakenly understood as wholesome and created by the hippies who gained control of Madison Avenue, who, incidentally, can no longer be bothered to keep track of what constitutes the term. In many cases, it seems as if *organic* means any fruit or vegetable that is not within three feet of a sewage treatment plant. Ultimately, the system is a cover-up for a large dating ring, in which backward, socially inept farmers find dates with cool inner-city chicks who have no clue about real nutrition. Ultimately, these confused women move on to other dating ruses like cults or the Libertarian Party.

ORIGINAL SIN:
THE NOTION THAT MANKIND, OWING TO BEING BORN OF THE ACT OF FORNICATION, IS INHERENTLY SINFUL BY NATURE. AT LEAST IF THEY'RE DOING IT RIGHT.

ORWELL, GEORGE:

TWENTIETH-CENTURY ENGLISH AUTHOR WHOSE MOST FAMOUS WORKS, *ANIMAL FARM* AND *1984*, CRITICIZE CONFORMITY AND FORESAW A FUTURE OVERRUN BY A TORTUROUS TOTALITARIAN STATE. LITTLE DID HE KNOW THAT 1984 WOULD ACTUALLY BRING ABOUT FAR MORE HORRIFIC EVENTS, SUCH AS THE INTRODUCTION OF THE UNWIELDY THREE-AND-A-HALF-INCH FLOPPY DISK, FOUR MORE YEARS WITH A MOVIE STAR AS PRESIDENT, AND A FRIGHTENING TRAIN WRECK OF A CELEBRITY CHARITY VIDEO CALLED "DO THEY KNOW IT'S CHRISTMAS?"

OUTSIDE THE BOX: A phrase to indicate unconventional thinking that is most commonly used by cripplingly dull people who are so incapable of being unconventional themselves that they still use tired old phrases like *outside the box.*

OVEN: A home appliance that is more successfully powered with electricity as opposed to gas; not so much in the interests of energy efficiency, but so that there will be one less thing around to use in the event that you decide to end it all.

OVER: Concluded, finished. Much like dial-up, typewriters, and common freaking courtesy.

OVERZEALOUS: Really, really excited about probably failing.

The Official Dictionary of Sarcasm

PAGE:

1. SOMETHING YOU CAN TELL YOUR GRANDCHILDREN YOU ONCE TURNED IN THE DAYS WHEN THERE WERE THINGS CALLED BOOKS. 2. A YOUNG PERSON EMPLOYED BY THE U.S. CONGRESS TO PROVIDE MESSENGER SERVICE, ADMINISTRATIVE SUPPORT, AND TRAGIC, PAINFUL, FORBIDDEN LONGING.

PAIN: Severe discomfort of a physical or emotional nature, such as occurs when accidentally whacking one's thumb with a hammer, being left by a lover, or having to suffer through the nonstop Christmas music that plays in retail establishments from the day after Halloween until December 24.

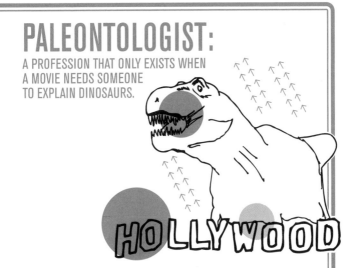

PALEONTOLOGIST:
A PROFESSION THAT ONLY EXISTS WHEN A MOVIE NEEDS SOMEONE TO EXPLAIN DINOSAURS.

PAPER: 1. A material that is no longer worth the paper it is printed on. 2. Something you write in college to prove to your professor that you are capable of regurgitating all the useless crap you ingested all semester.

PARANOID: The feeling that the feeling that everybody is out to get you may not be just a feeling.

PARENTS: The two people you least want to picture doing the nasty, even though you wouldn't be here if the nasty had not been done.

The Official Dictionary of Sarcasm

PARK: Something a city puts up so that its citizens can temporarily forget they live in a filthy, crime-infested hellhole by strolling through a *green* filthy, crime-infested hellhole with squirrels.

PARKING: The selfless act of graciously leaving one's car to be potentially stolen or vandalized.

PARKING GARAGE: The only enclosed area with prominently displayed signs regarding chemicals known to cause cancer that nonetheless continues to attract motorists by the thousands.

PARKING GARAGE ATTENDANT:

A PERSON WHO GETS PAID TO GIVE YOU ONLY THE BAREST INDICATION OF YOUR EXISTENCE WHILE HE OR SHE CATCHES UP ON EITHER SOME READING OR DAYTIME TELEVISION.

PARTHENON, THE: Ancient Greek temple erected in the fifth century BC as an offering to the goddess Athena, who you can bet also got custody of the kids and the beach house in the Hamptons.

PARTY:

1. A SOCIAL GATHERING AT WHICH EVERYBODY NEEDS TO GET DRUNK TO DEAL WITH HOW MUCH THEY HATE BEING SOCIAL. 2. A POLITICAL GROUP FORMED TO GAIN POWER IN OFFICE. USUALLY CONSISTS OF EITHER RICH, CALLOUS MONEY-GRUBBERS WHO ARE OUT TO DESTROY THE PLANET AND WOULD PREFER IT IF POOR PEOPLE WOULD SIMPLY DIE OR RICH, NAÏVE MONEY-GRUBBERS WHO WON'T BE HAPPY UNTIL THE GOVERNMENT PAYS FOR EVERYTHING FROM YOUR HEALTH CARE TO YOUR GROCERIES, EVERYBODY IS HAVING SEX IN THE STREET, AND PEOPLE ARE ALLOWED TO MARRY FARM ANIMALS.

PASSWORD: Once a badass clandestine phrase used to gain admittance into an illegal drinking or gaming establishment; now a case-sensitive, goofy reference to one's pet, favorite sports team, or movie that is used to gain admittance to the clandestine thrill of paying your gas bill online.

PASTA:
A STARCH WITH SOME OF THE FUNNIEST NAMES IN THE HISTORY OF FOOD.

PATIENT: The quality of being calm and tolerant during a maddeningly frustrating time. Hardly a surprise, then, that this term is also used to describe people in society who are unfortunate enough to require medical attention.

PAYCHECK: A piece of paper with a bunch of numbers on it that magically becomes the future profits of Kmart, the dog track, or a concubine, depending on one's proclivities.

PEACE: Something that sounds good in principle, but really is just not healthy for the economy.

PEACHY: A word uttered through clenched teeth to describe a situation that is really not peachy at all.

PEANUT BUTTER: A substance which, combined with monthly direct-deposits from your parents, allowed you to get through college.

PEDESTRIAN:
A MOVING TARGET.

PENCIL IN: Postpone indefinitely.

PENIS:

The male brain.

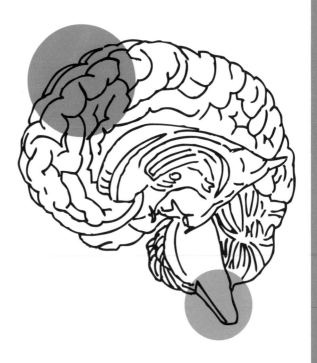

PEOPLE: The humans with whom we are forced to share the planet; for the most part, we are never aware of this mass of humanity existing all around us except when they leave an unwanted pubic hair behind to be found by the next person who uses the bus station bathroom.

PERFECTIONIST: The worst kind of boss; the best kind of sex partner.

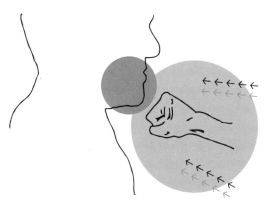

PERKY:
LIVELY, JAUNTY, BRISK, OR, TO PUT IT ANOTHER WAY, JUST ASKING FOR A PUNCH IN THE DAMN FACE.

PERVERTED: A word used to indignantly describe an abhorrent sexual practice that you might like to try.

PESSIMIST: Someone who cannot look at a threshing machine without thinking that he or she is destined to fall into it.

PGA:

PROFESSIONAL GOLFERS' ASSOCIATION. AN ORGANIZATION DEVOTED TO CHAMPIONING THE WORLD'S MOST NONDESCRIPT PANTS.

PHOTOCOPIER: An office machine that malfunctions so often that the phrase "just walk away and leave it for the next person to deal with" should be included in its owner's manual.

PHOTOGRAPH:

AN IRREFUTABLE VISUAL RECORD OF THE FACT THAT BETWEEN THE AGES OF ELEVEN AND FIFTEEN, YOU LOOKED LIKE A TOTAL DORK.

PHOTOGRAPHER: In the case of a portrait photographer, the person you pay to give you pictures of you and the kids that nobody really wants; in the case of a wedding photographer, the person you pay to give you pictures you will never have time to look at again.

PICASSO, PABLO: Legendary twentieth-century painter whose canvases reveal that his many lovers apparently had three or more breasts and noses where their eyes should be.

PIGEON: A CREATURE THAT REPAYS YOUR KINDNESS IN FEEDING IT BREAD CRUMBS FROM A PARK BENCH BY CRAPPING ON ALL YOUR FAVORITE BUILDINGS.

PILOT:

A PLEASANTLY INEBRIATED CHAP WHOM YOU HAPPILY
ENTRUST WITH MAKING SURE YOU DON'T PLUMMET TO
YOUR DEATH.

PIMP: An often distasteful and even abusive figure who makes a living callously farming out a stable of luckless whores, but whose charmingly garish lifestyle makes a delightful fashion statement for one's wardrobe, automobile, or den!

PIPE: For one group of men, a dignified container for tobacco, meant to be smoked in one's study with one's golden retriever lounging at one's feet; for another group of men, an often-clogged device meant to be smoked in one's bedroom with one's Phish and Weezer MP3s blaring from one's iPod dock.

PIRATE:

1. A SNAPPY AND ECLECTIC DRESSER WHO USES PLUNDERING ON THE HIGH SEAS AS AN EXCUSE TO AVOID COMING OUT OF THE CLOSET. 2. TO BRAZENLY AND ILLEGALLY PROCURE A VISUAL OR AUDIO RECORDING, KNOWING FULL WELL IT COULD DEPRIVE A PHALANX OF MULTIMILLIONAIRES OF ANYTHING FROM EIGHT TO NINE CENTS.

PITY: An emotion that allows us to feel we have concern for the misfortune of others, when in fact we are simply glad we did not get dealt the God-awful hand they did.

PIZZA: A tasty way to avail yourself of the four basic food groups: fat, fat, fat, and fat.

PLATO: Ancient Greek writer and thinker; Plato was among those who developed the foundations of philosophy in the Western world. So thank him the next time you wake up in a cold sweat wondering why the hell we're all here.

PLAYSTATION: A company dedicated to wiping out any semblance of social skills in children within the next ten years.

PLEASE: A supposedly polite term that children tend to repeat ad nauseam while tugging on your pant leg.

PLEASURE: The nagging sense that you will be punished for feeling so damn good.

PLUMBER:

THE PROFESSION WHOSE UNIQUE DISTINCTION IS BEING THE ONE JOB EVERYBODY REFERS TO WHEN THEY ARE UNHAPPY WITH THEIR CAREER CHOICE AND WISTFULLY SPEAK OF WHAT SIMPLE, UNCOMPLICATED, AND PROFITABLE PURSUIT THEY MIGHT HAVE CHOSEN TO DO INSTEAD.

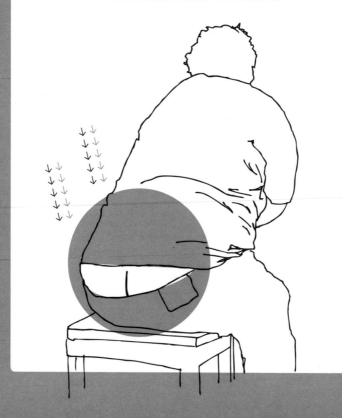

PLUNGER:

A DEVICE SPECIFICALLY DESIGNED TO GIVE YOU THREE HOURS' WORTH OF HOPEFUL GURGLING/SUCKING NOISES THAT ALL SEEM TO BE THE BEGINNINGS OF A BREAKTHROUGH UNTIL YOU FINALLY GIVE UP AND CALL THE PLUMBER.

PMS: A condition that is linked to the cycles of the moon so profoundly that every twenty-eight days it turns a perfectly mild-mannered girlfriend into a werewolf.

PODCAST: A revolutionary way to offer an audio or video version of what you do to the same 250 million people who ignored your blog.

POEM: That one lame-ass excursion into your subconscious that you are too embarrassed to show anybody but refuse to destroy, in the hopes that after you are dead someone will find it tucked into your high school yearbook and realize how damn deep you were.

POKER: Proof that men are so desperate for excuses to smoke, drink, and pass gas together that they are even willing to lose a substantial amount of money to do it.

POLE: A rounded metal support used by professional dancers at those times when the extra weight of a very heavy G-string makes them more prone to losing their balance.

POLITICIAN: A person who inspires such inherent distrust that we feel perfectly comfortable letting him or her make a whole bunch of important decision for us.

POOR: A lacking in material wealth that is often said to be a happier state of existence, wherein one is unencumbered and able to find happiness in what is truly important. And boy, are rich people more than glad to let a world full of deluded suckers buy into this crap.

POPULAR: Well liked by a large group of people. And, if there is any justice, ending up pumping gas and living in a trailer park twenty years after they are elected most likely to succeed.

POP-UP: 1. A type of three-dimensional picture book designed to give children an added level of engagement with a subject. 2. A type of two-dimensional Internet advertising designed to give adults an added level of fury-induced embolism.

PORN:

A DEPICTION OF SEXUAL CONGRESS ON FILM THAT FEATURES APPROXIMATELY ELEVEN HUNDRED TIMES MORE HIGH-PITCHED SQUEALS OF PROFANITY THAN ACTUALLY OCCUR DURING NORMAL LOVEMAKING.

POST OFFICE: A place where customers have the option of either waiting in line for an agent or doing their business with a machine, since there is a fifty-fifty chance the latter will provide a far more personable experience.

POTATO: A simple tuberous vegetable that was doing quite well on its own for centuries and then suffered a series of indignities, most notably au gratin, the shameless mark-up of its skins as an appetizer, and a toy company that decided it would be good to make one with a bunch of plastic stick-on facial features.

POTTER, HARRY: The lead boy wizard in a fantasy book franchise that took the world by storm, despite the fact that it obviously contains coded messages from Satan about how to disembowel your best friend.

POWER LUNCH:
A STRATEGIC SESSION OF MANIPULATION AND PREPARATION FOR EVENTUAL BACKSTABBING ARRANGED AROUND A PLEASANT NOONTIME MEAL.

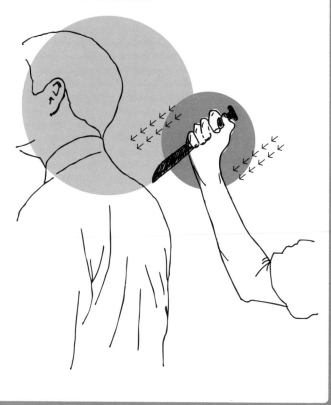

POWER NAP:

A SHORT AMOUNT OF SLEEP TAKEN DURING BUSINESS HOURS SO THAT ONE CAN AWAKEN DISORIENTED, FOGGY, AND OUT OF IT, NEVER REALLY COMING BACK TO ANY LEVEL OF EFFECTIVENESS FOR THE REST OF THE DAY.

POWERPOINT: A multimedia presentational tool that uses slides, charts, even animation and sound effects to bore the stuffing out of your audience even more effectively than they would be bored by just you.

PRECIOUS: Code word meaning "intolerable." Used when referring to such things as a small child's attempt at ballet or any human-interest story airing on National Public Radio.

PRESCHOOL:

AN EDUCATIONAL ESTABLISHMENT WHOSE SOLE PURPOSE IS TO BACK UP TRAFFIC BY SIX OR SEVEN BLOCKS WHILE A BUNCH OF HYBRID-DRIVING NOUVEAU YUPPIES WHO ARE TOO LAZY TO PARK AND WALK BACK FOR THEIR CHILDREN SIT THERE BLOCKING THE ROADWAY WAITING FOR THEIR IDIOT PROGENY TO SHOW THEMSELVES.

PRESIDENT: A person appointed by the American people to screw up the country for a period of four years. Or, if the screwing is really going well, eight years.

PRESLEY, ELVIS:

THE KING OF ROCK 'N' ROLL. HIS CAREER WAS TRAGICALLY CUT SHORT BY AN ADDICTION TO BARBITURATES, WHICH HE FOUND NECESSARY TO START TAKING AFTER THE TRAUMA OF SHAKING HANDS WITH RICHARD NIXON.

The Official Dictionary of Sarcasm

PRIEST: A man who goes through years of devotional training to make you feel bad for doing all the things he is not allowed to do.

PRINCE, THE: Reactionary treatise written in 1513 by Niccolò Machiavelli. It advocates all manner of cruelty in the obtaining and keeping of political power. This decidedly retro nonsense is nonetheless still part of the mindset of many a despotic leader today and is evidenced in everything from waterboarding to no more free doughnuts in the Monday meeting.

PRISON: A place where a person can get some much-needed downtime.

PRIVATE DETECTIVE: A hopelessly bored man who spends his life waiting in vain for a routine investigation to lead to a giant murder conspiracy involving powerful and influential people, one of whom is a socialite femme fatale who instigates a torrid affair only to double-cross him in the end, leaving him cynical and alone in an unforgiving world.

PROBABLY: Unlikely. As in, *"I'm sure I will probably be able to come to your* M*A*S*H *theme party."*

PRODIGAL SON: As originally described in the Gospel story, the prodigal son is a man who wastes his family's money on loose living and is celebrated upon returning, thus angering his older brother, who stayed at home and did good deeds. The boys' father then explains that it is more important that the son came to his senses than it is for him to be punished. Unfortunately, what the parable does not go on to explain is how the older brother had to grit his teeth and swallow fistfuls of resentful bile, which resulted in premature hardening of the arteries and death. Some reports even indicate that dad and the younger brother had a good laugh about this, although these are unsubstantiated.

PROFESSIONAL: A word inserted before any number of occupational titles to imply a level of competence that is, for the most part, very pointedly not in evidence.

PROFESSOR: Someone who has to deal with students in order to pay off a student loan.

PROFIT: The money a corporation sets aside for hot tubs and hookers.

PROMISCUOUS: The aspect of your past that gets downgraded to serial monogamy on your online dating profile.

PROSTITUTE:

THE ONLY PROFESSION BESIDES ROLLER-SKATING BURGER-JOINT WAITRESS THAT INVOLVES REPEATEDLY LEANING INTO CAR WINDOWS JUST TO GET THINGS GOING.

PSYCHEDELIC: Characterized by hallucinatory images or altered states of consciousness. Co-opted as a visual style by clothing designers and filmmakers who want to create a fun, kicky vibe out of those madcap days when a bunch of nutty kids were overdosing on heroin.

PSYCHOPATH: A criminally antisocial personality that remains a source of fascination to normal people, who wonder whether somewhere inside them lurks the capacity to suck someone's brains out with a straw.

PUBLIC RESTROOM: A place containing toilet seats that make you wish you could be taught how to hover.

PYRAMIDS, THE:

WONDERS OF ANCIENT EGYPT, THE PYRAMIDS WERE BUILT AS TOMBS TO THE PHARAOHS. WHILE IT WAS SUPPOSEDLY AN ALMOST SUPERNATURAL ACHIEVEMENT FOR PEOPLE THOUSANDS OF YEARS AGO TO BUILD THESE THINGS, IT COULDN'T HAVE BEEN THAT HARD BECAUSE THERE'S A REALLY AWESOME ONE IN LAS VEGAS NOW, AND NO ONE HAS TO GO TO DUSTY OLD NORTH AFRICA TO SEE IT, EITHER.

The Official Dictionary of Sarcasm

PYTHON, MONTY: British comedy troupe that enjoyed the peak of popularity in the 1970s but lives on, rather sadly and tragically, in that one friend everyone has— the one who insists on launching into a painfully embarrassing, full-on reenactment of the dead-parrot sketch or the Black Knight scene from *Holy Grail* at the slightest provocation.

QUAINT: Pleasingly old-fashioned. Like the shops in a small town, a wise old saying, or someone who deliberately remains a virgin past the age of twenty-five.

QUALIFIED: Having obtained just enough advanced degrees or training to completely foul things up.

QUALITY: Designed to wear out in eight months instead of six.

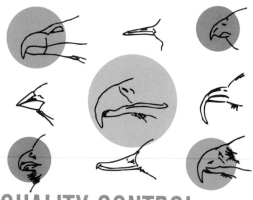

QUALITY CONTROL:
THE DEPARTMENT THAT ENSURES YOUR MEAT CONTAINS ONLY THE FEDERALLY MANDATED MINIMUM OF BEAKS, HOOVES, FUR, BONE FRAGMENTS, PESTICIDES, HORMONES, DISEASE-CARRYING PARASITES, AND FLAVOR.

QUEEN:

BRITISH ROCK GROUP POPULAR IN THE 1970S WHOSE SONG "WE WILL ROCK YOU" HAS BECOME A STAPLE AT SPORTING EVENTS, WHERE HUNDREDS OF AGGRESSIVELY HETEROSEXUAL MEN DO NOT STOP TO THINK THAT THE SONG GETTING THEM PUMPED IS BEING SUNG BY A MAN WHO THOUGHT NOTHING OF WEARING A CROP TOP AND TIGHT PINK HOT PANTS.

QUEEN, THE: The most prominent figurehead of British royalty and part of a long line of privileged people who think the sun shines out of their butt cracks.

QUEER: A word that used to mean anything out of the ordinary and now means anyone who is ordinarily out.

QUICKEN: A personal finance software designed to easily and efficiently guide you toward the realization that you may soon have to sell off one of your children.

QUIRKY:
ALL-PURPOSE WORD USED TO COVER UP THE IRRITATINGLY INANE. *"BOY, THAT FRIEND OF YOURS WHO NEVER SHUTS UP AND DRESSES LIKE SOMETHING OUT OF DESPERATELY SEEKING SUSAN SURE IS QUIRKY!"*

QUITTER: Someone who has finally come to his or her senses.

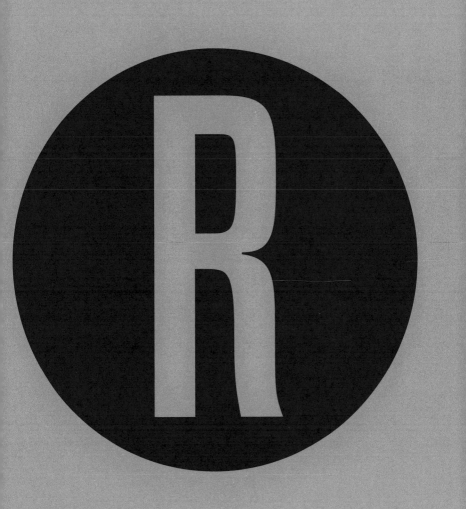

RABBI:

A LEARNED MAN WELL VERSED IN THE LAWS OF HIS FAITH, WHO NONETHELESS SEEMS TO KEEP WALKING INTO A BAR WITH A PRIEST AND A MINISTER.

RADIO: A once-proud medium now so overrun by blowhards and overproduced hip-hop that one wishes one had been born with earlids.

RAM: Random-access memory. Something one apparently has in one's hard drive, although nobody ever remembers how much they have or how to find out how much they have, unless they happen to be around the one friend who understands computers while wondering aloud about whether they have enough room to download Adobe Flash Player.

REALITY: A state in which you assume everybody else resides, until you start dating.

RECEIPT: Proof that you have purchased a really crappy gift that someone will most likely want to return.

RECEPTIONIST: Someone who would prefer it if you would go away.

RED SQUARE:
WORLD-FAMOUS RUSSIAN CITY SQUARE IN THE SHADOW OF THE KREMLIN. SURROUNDED BY A VAST INFRASTRUCTURE OF ROADWAYS, AS WELL AS THE INSPIRING, COLORFUL, ONION-DOMED ST. BASIL'S CATHEDRAL. HONESTLY, YOU CAN HARDLY BELIEVE A BUNCH OF DIRTY COMMIES CAME UP WITH SOMETHING SO AWESOME.

REGRET: The gnawing, inescapable feeling that behaving like a total dick for your entire life may not have been such a good idea.

RELATIONSHIP: An agreement to no longer share the information that you are seeing other people.

RELIGION:

AN INSTITUTION FOUNDED ON THE WORSHIP OF A SET OF SHARED BELIEFS. ALTHOUGH IF YOU'RE INVOLVED IN ONE THAT MAINTAINS EARTH WAS FOUNDED BY A RACE OF SUPER-INTELLIGENT SPACE ALIENS, YOU MAY WANT TO RECONSIDER FORKING OVER ANY MORE OPERATING FUNDS THE NEXT TIME THEY PASS THE COLLECTION PLATE.

REMOTE:

THE ONLY BATTERY-POWERED APPLIANCE THAT CARRIES WITH IT THE FIVE STAGES OF GRIEF. DENIAL: *"I AM NOT SIMPLY USING THIS REMOTE AS A WAY TO GAIN POWER OVER MY WIFE OR GIRLFRIEND."* ANGER: *"MY REMOTE. MINE!"* BARGAINING: *"WHAT IF WE JUST WATCHED NASCAR TOGETHER?"* DEPRESSION: *"FINE. WAITING TO EXHALE. SEE IF I CARE."* ACCEPTANCE: *"HONEY, I'M READY TO CHANGE ALL THE PRESETS."*

RENT: A monthly occurrence that demonstrates how readily one can get blood from a stone.

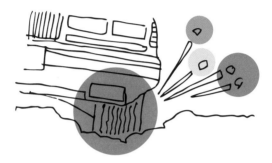

RENTAL CAR:
A VEHICLE THAT MAKES YOU SEEK OUT POTHOLES.

REPLY ALL: An e-mail function that immediately copies all the contacts of the original sender when a response is sent, subjecting them to rants about his or her political views or take on current events, or how the original e-mail was a hoax. This presupposes a level of caring on the part of all the copied recipients that is simply not there, since most of them glance just long enough at the reply to realize that they do not know or cannot stand the douche who sent it and happily hit "delete."

RESOLUTION, NEW YEAR'S:

A FRESH RESOLVE ABOUT CHANGING OR IMPROVING AN ASPECT OF ONE'S LIFE THAT KICKS IN EVERY JANUARY 1 AND USUALLY BITES THE DUST AFTER AN EATING BINGE, BENDER, OR ORGY ON JANUARY 2.

RESTAURANT:

A PLACE THAT GIVES YOU THE NAGGING SUSPICION THAT, DESPITE THE PROMINENTLY DISPLAYED SIGNS IN THE RESTROOM, EMPLOYEES ARE NOT WASHING THEIR HANDS BEFORE RETURNING TO WORK.

RETAIL SALES CLERK: Apathy with a name tag.

RETAIL STORE: The backbone of a merchandise-based economy, the retail store has gone through significant changes since its glory days in the early- to mid-twentieth century, when specialized, learned salespeople would inform each customer about the merits of a given product and an air of servitude and grace pervaded the premises. Quite different from the modern experience, in which one wanders around aisles of discarded tube socks—passing clerks who avoid eye contact for fear of having to actually assist you—and waits in long lines behind cashiers, who go into anaphylactic shock when the price scanner malfunctions.

RHYTHM:
SOMETHING POSSESSED BY A TOTAL OF SEVEN WHITE PEOPLE.

The Official Dictionary of Sarcasm

RICE: A starchy side dish served with Chinese food, without which we would not be aware that we have eaten anything at all.

RICH: Either someone having significant material wealth or something having significant amounts of butter, eggs, and cream. Both of which sort of kill you in very different ways.

RIGHT: 1. A political stance marked by firm positions on traditional values and lower taxes and by wishing there could be a giant, invisible force field that would keep out the foreigners. 2. Something that is due a person; for example, the right to free speech, the right to bear arms, or the right to shoot someone who does not believe in free speech.

RING: A metal circular band placed on the third finger of the left hand that lets everyone know you are married, thus inexplicably making you that much more sexy and attractive to lustful strangers.

RINGTONE: A sound effect or musical sample chosen by cellular phone users to express their individuality. What most of them do not know is that when their phone kicks in with the theme from *Shaft*, the reason people stare has very little to do with admiration.

ROCKET SCIENCE: Much like brain surgery, what most of the stuff you do is not.

ROLLING STONES, THE:
LEGENDARY BRITISH ROCK 'N' ROLLERS WHOSE CONTINUING LIVE PERFORMANCES WOULD NOT HAVE BEEN POSSIBLE WITHOUT FORMALDEHYDE.

ROMANCE: 1. The ardent feelings associated with love, which can be said to have worn off right around the time you became comfortable peeing with the door open. 2. A style of novel in which women are able to find men who look like Fabio and are not only able to find their G-spot but can actually string a sentence together.

ROMANCE, OFFICE: Something that is naughty and fun for all of five minutes, after which both parties realize that "Don't poop where you eat" is a pretty solid little motto.

ROTARY: 1. Mysterious humanitarian organization that claims to spread goodwill around the world and yet continues to allow low-rent weddings and bad comedians to occupy some of the tackiest wood-paneled function rooms known to man. 2. A circular traffic junction designed to frighten out-of-towners.

RUBBERS: Once a common term for galoshes, now a common term for prophylactics. Proving once again that the size of one's feet may well correlate to the size of one's penis.

RUNNER: A person who will not rest until they have personally funded the summer home of their knee surgeon.

RUTH, BABE:

BASEBALL LEGEND AND POWER HITTER FOR BOTH THE BOSTON RED SOX AND NEW YORK YANKEES, AND THE ONLY PLAYER IN HISTORY TO CREDIT HIS ATHLETIC PROWESS TO A STEADY REGIMEN OF CIGARS, HARD LIQUOR, AND WOMEN.

RUT-RO:

THE PHRASE *UH-OH*, AS UTTERED BY THE POPULAR CARTOON CHARACTER SCOOBY-DOO AND USED WITH ALARMING FREQUENCY BY THE SAME COWORKERS WHO SAY "I'LL BE BACK" IN A BAD SCHWARZENEGGER ACCENT WHEN THEY ARE GOING TO USE THE BATHROOM.

SACRIFICE: To go without a third Cape Cod summer home to make sure the children do not have to attend public school.

SADIST: One who gets pleasure out of cruelty, such as the tone-deaf boyfriend, girlfriend, or spouse who insists on caterwauling along to the car radio on long road trips while you sit cringing and numb in the passenger seat.

SAINT AUGUSTINE: Fourth-century theologian whose thirteen books of confessions were so damn juicy that he became one of the cornerstones of Christianity.

SALAD: Just another example of how having to lose thirty pounds or be at risk for heart disease and stroke has made it impossible to enjoy life.

SALAD BAR: A trough for humans.

SALT: A substance available in small paper packets that is dropped into your bag of take-out food in case the eleven hundred milligrams of sodium in your cheeseburger was not quite enough.

SANTA CLAUS:

1. A JOLLY, ROTUND FELLOW WHOSE WHOLESOME IMAGE AS A BELOVED CHILDREN'S FIGURE IS SOMEWHAT UNDERMINED BY THE FACT THAT HE MUST BE ON CRACK TO BE ABLE TO PERSONALLY DELIVER GIFTS TO NEARLY SEVEN BILLION PEOPLE IN ROUGHLY NINE HOURS. 2. A MAN EMPLOYED BY A MALL TO BREATHE THE SMELL OF BEER ONTO CHILDREN.

SARTRE, JEAN PAUL: Twentieth-century existentialist writer who, in his famous treatise *Being and Nothingness*, posited that all of us live with the dichotomy of existing within a lack of consciousness whereas in order to be alive, we must nonetheless make conscious choices—just before his head exploded.

SAVVY: A word used on résumés (for example, *Internet savvy*) to indicate that you are completely clueless on a subject and have no intention of learning it until three days after you are hired.

SCANDAL: An often immoral incident that results in disgrace and humiliation for the parties involved while delivering big fun, titillation, and sexually frank material read by traditionally boring news anchors to the rest of us.

SCHOOL:

A PLACE TO LEAVE ONE'S GUNS AND KNIVES WHILE SPENDING THE DAY DISCUSSING *SILAS MARNER* AND ATTEMPTING LONG DIVISION.

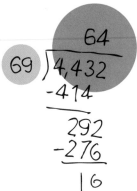

SCHWARZENEGGER, ARNOLD:

MAYBE NOT THE FIRST ACTOR-TURNED-POLITICIAN WHO OWES HIS CAREER TO STEROIDS, BUT CERTAINLY THE ONLY ONE WHO LOOKS IT.

SCIENCE: The study and investigation of phenomena based on rigorous study and experiment, conducted solely for the purposes of pissing off those who think God did it all.

SCIENTIST:

A PERSON IN A LAB COAT WHO APPEARS AT THE BEGINNING OF SCIENCE FICTION FILMS TO EXPLAIN HOW THE COLLISION OF CERTAIN ISOTOPES CAN RESULT IN A HALF-MAN-HALF-LEMUR.

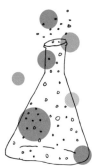

SCREENSAVER: An image chosen to fill one's computer screen when the computer is not in use. Often, inexplicably, a picture of one's family, as if dealing with their unceasing demands on your time in three-dimensional space wasn't quite enough.

SECRETARY OF STATE: A person who, on a local level, helps to officiate elections, register businesses, and register automobiles and who, on a national level, gets to have people killed.

SECURITY GUARD: A person who is about as much a deterrent to crime as leaving a radio on in the house while you're on vacation.

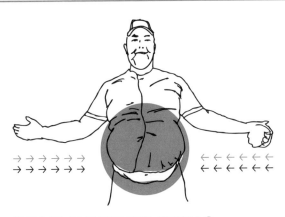

SELF-DEPRECATING:
POINTING OUT ONE'S OWN ENORMOUS CATALOG OF HIGHLY ANNOYING SHORTCOMINGS TO SAVE OTHERS THE BOTHER OF DOING SO.

SELF-DESTRUCTIVE: Taking steps to hasten one's demise to save others the bother of doing so.

SELF-DISCIPLINED: Making the rest of us look bad.

SELF-EFFACING: Acting in such a way as to not call any attention to oneself to save others the bother of paying attention to you.

SEMESTER ABROAD: A chance to lose one's virginity to the son or daughter of the kindly German host family that is letting you stay in their guest room.

SEND: The button you should have thought a little longer about hitting before firing off that e-mail that was the written equivalent of a drunk dial.

SENILE: A word whose definition you will no longer be able to recall by the time it applies to you.

SENSITIVE: Having a tendency to get all bent out of shape just because somebody calls you a barely sentient troglodyte.

SENSUAL: A lesser form of *sexy* that implies all sorts of creepy tactile experience and delight of the senses and all that garbage instead of just going straight to ripping off clothing and going at it like rutting antelopes.

SEX: 1. One's gender; the designation of the physical attributes of being either male or female. 2. Putting those attributes to the best possible use.

SHAKESPEARE, WILLIAM:

SIXTEENTH- AND EARLY-SEVENTEENTH-CENTURY PLAYWRIGHT WIDELY CONSIDERED TO BE THE FINEST DRAMATIST EVER TO WORK IN THE ENGLISH LANGUAGE. WHICH IS WEIRD, SINCE ANY ENGLISH-SPEAKING PERSON WHO HAS HAD TO READ OR SIT THROUGH ONE OF THIS DUDE'S PLAYS WILL TELL YOU THAT YOU CAN'T UNDERSTAND A THING ANYBODY IS SAYING.

SHAME: The realization that nobody else thinks the thing you were caught doing was as wholesome as you thought as was.

SHATNER, WILLIAM:

SO-CALLED ACTOR FROM CANADA, MOST FAMOUS FOR HIS PORTRAYAL OF CAPTAIN JAMES T. KIRK ON THE ORIGINAL *STAR TREK*, THOUGH VERY LITTLE ACTING WAS REQUIRED FOR HIS ROLE, WHICH LARGELY INVOLVED MAKING LOVE TO ALIEN WOMEN WHO REPRESENTED ANY NUMBER OF GALAXIES AND FEATURED VARIOUS ELABORATE HEADDRESSES, DAY-GLO SKIN TONES, AND ANYWHERE FROM THREE TO EIGHT BREASTS.

SHOES: Footwear sold largely in retail outlets and, much like with the purchase of gasoline, an experience that has gone from full-service to self-service. Which may not be such a bad thing, depending on how you feel about a guy with BO and a comb-over grasping the back of your ankles while you sit helplessly in a very low-slung chair.

SHOPPING: Slow death. Wasting six or seven perfectly good hours looking at stuff while shuffling along at an infuriatingly slow pace that brings to mind the denizens of a nursing home on their way from their rooms to a game of Pokeno. How this brain-deadening way to spend a day came to qualify as an "activity" remains a mystery, especially to those who endured it just to be nice that one time when they first started dating.

SHOWER: 1. God's way of saying that if you want to be clean, sooner or later you will have to see yourself naked. 2. A gathering of women revolving around either an impending wedding or impending birth, usually in that order.

SINATRA, FRANK: Legendary twentieth-century American song stylist often rumored to have ties to organized crime. As such, it would probably be unwise to say anything sarcastic about him.

SISTER: 1. A female sibling; also known as someone who really knows how to push your buttons. And damned if she doesn't do it every time you get together. 2. A nun; also known as someone who can ask God to push your buttons if she wants to.

SKIN: Sole means of support for the lotion industry.

SKYDIVING:
PLUNGING TO ONE'S DEATH, INTERRUPTED.

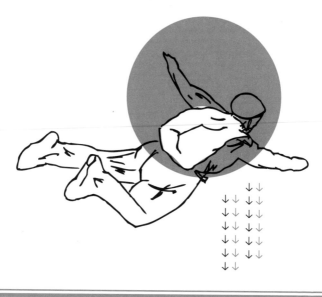

SLACKER: A term that attempts to graft an air of coolness onto being a lazy bastard.

SLOCUM, JOSHUA:

SETTING SAIL FROM NEW ENGLAND IN APRIL OF 1895 AND RETURNING THREE YEARS LATER, SLOCUM BECAME THE FIRST MAN TO COMPLETE A SOLO SEA VOYAGE AROUND THE WORLD. HERE, THEN, WAS A MAN DRIVEN ONWARD BY HIS DETERMINATION TO BRING NEW AND INCREDIBLY RESISTANT STRAINS OF VD BACK TO HIS COUNTRYMEN.

SLUT: A vexing example of the inherent sexism still running rampant in our society, *slut* is a word for which is there is *no* male equivalent; and certainly not one that even comes close to implying the same level of skankiness.

SOCIAL NETWORKING:
A WAY OF IMAGINING THAT YOU STILL HAVE SOCIAL SKILLS AND CAN NETWORK EVEN THOUGH YOU ARE SURGICALLY ATTACHED TO YOUR COMPUTER AND NEVER LEAVE YOUR HOUSE.

SOCRATES: Philosopher of classical Greece, whose criticism of society so angered the authorities that he was sentenced to death by hemlock. This is a far cry from the social critics of today, who are usually sentenced to death by Fox News.

SOFA: An item of furniture made a household necessity by the National Alliance of Deadbeat Friends.

SON: Someone a father keeps on hand for those times when he doesn't feel disappointed enough.

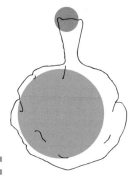

SOPHOMORIC:

WHAT YOU CALL A FART JOKE WHEN YOU DON'T WANT TO ADMIT IT WAS FREAKING HILARIOUS.

SORDID: Wretched. Squalid. Degrading. What's not to like?

SOUP: The culinary equivalent of taking a bath in one's own filth, soup is a way of offering your dinner guests a heaping bowlful of everything in your fridge that was about an hour away from becoming rancid. Yum!

SPAM:
PORK SHOULDER MEAT, HAM, AND GELATINOUS OOZE IN A CAN. IS AMERICA A GREAT COUNTRY, OR WHAT?

SPAM: Unsolicited e-mail. Proof of the existence of something even more heinous than the product it is named after.

SPECIAL: Appearing with much more frequency in the latter part of the twentieth century as part of the movement to boost self-esteem in preadolescents, *special* is something teachers were encouraged to begin calling every child in their class, even though statistically most of them are painfully ordinary losers who will never grow up to be Mozart and in fact find it an almost Herculean task just to make a turkey by tracing their hand on a piece of construction paper.

SPEED BUMP:

1. A RAISED ASPHALT RIDGE PUT ACROSS A SECTION OF ROAD TO PISS OFF DRIVERS WHO ARE NOW FORCED TO MISS THE CHANCE TO RUN DOWN AN INNOCENT PERSON.
2. A HITCH OR A GLITCH IN ONE'S DAILY LIFE OR BUSINESS. USUALLY CALLED SO BY THE IDIOT WHO CAUSED THE GLITCH AND WANTS TO MAKE A PATHETIC ATTEMPT AT DOWNPLAYING HIS OR HER INCOMPETENCE BY REFERRING TO IT AS NOTHING MORE THAN AN ADORABLE LITTLE BUMP IN THE ROAD. SCHMUCK.

The Official Dictionary of Sarcasm

SPHINX, THE: Giant stone statue of a lion with a human head. Clearly, the ancient Egyptians had access to some very interesting mushrooms.

SPIDER-MAN: Comic book character noted for being the first of a hip, new style of hero with everyday, perfectly normal, real life problems, like unrequited love, being indirectly responsible for the death of one's uncle, and an entire city full of freakish, pathological, costumed supervillains bent on your destruction.

SPIN: 1. A reinterpretation of negative publicity that attempts to reframe things in a positive light. *"Yes, the Ambassador was found with a sheep, but this is because he would never think of trying such an abnormal act on a woman."* 2. A style of aerobics that lets you see what it would be like to have your bicycle ride narrated by a slightly effeminate boot camp drill instructor on methamphetamines.

SPORTSCASTER: Television personality who must consult a thesaurus prior to each broadcast to come up with more colorful ways to say the home team lost. Popular favorites include *crushed, trounced, annihilated, slaughtered, thrashed,* and even *drubbing* or *shellacking* if it has been a really bad week.

SPREADSHEET: Boredom in Excel form.

SPRING:

THE TIME OF YEAR WHEN A YOUNG MAN'S FANCY TURNS TO LOVE AND A YOUNG WOMAN'S FANCY TURNS TO PEPPER SPRAY.

SPRING BREAK: A week-long bacchanal that makes the reign of Caligula look like a scrapbooking party at the Red Hat Society.

SQUEAMISH:
LIKELY TO BLOW CHUNKS DURING WHAT THE REST OF US THINK ARE THE MOST AWESOME PARTS OF ZOMBIE MOVIES.

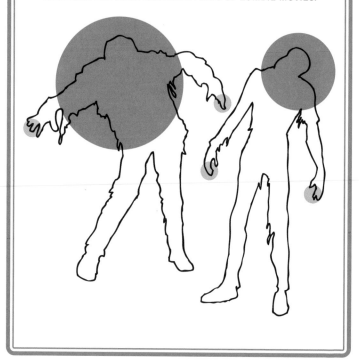

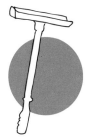

SQUEEGEE:
AN IMPLEMENT LEFT IN A PLASTIC BIN OF BLACKENED BILGE WATER BY THOUGHTFUL GAS STATION OWNERS SO THAT THEIR CUSTOMERS MAY APPLY A THIN FILM OF GRIME TO THEIR WINDSHIELD WHILE FUELING.

STALIN, JOSEPH: General secretary of the Communist Party in Russia from 1922 to 1953 and known for his Great Purge, in which anyone he suspected of treason was rounded up and killed or sent to labor camps in the Gulag. Apart from that, he was a pretty nice guy.

STAR TREK: The first entertainment-industry phenomenon known to prolong virginity.

STAR WARS: Blockbuster science fiction film released in 1977 that introduced a legion of fans to the concept of The Force, a power within each of us that can bring about a hoped-for outcome simply by concentrating hard enough. Of course, the only person in real life for whom this hokum actually works is George Lucas, who has hoped for an outcome of repeated generations of suckers shelling out for countless action figures and repeated lame-ass sequels. Obviously, he has gotten exactly what he wanted.

STATUE OF LIBERTY: Iconic statue of a robed, torch-bearing woman located in New York Harbor. A symbol of the way the United States extends a welcoming hand to the tired, poor, huddled masses from just about everywhere, with the possible exception of France, which, ironically, is where we got the damn thing from in the first place.

STAYCATION:

CONVINCING YOURSELF THAT SLEEPING LATE IN THE MORNING AND BURNING THROUGH BOXED SETS OF *THE SHIELD* AT NIGHT IS PREFERABLE TO THAT WEEK OF KAYAKING IN THE KOMODO ISLANDS, WHICH YOU CAN NO LONGER AFFORD.

STEREOTYPE: A pat classification of a group of people that is not allowed to be funny unless it is being acted out by someone who is a member of the group being stereotyped.

STIGMATA: A word that clueless people often use when they are talking about a social *stigma*, little knowing that their seemingly innocuous discussion on some aspect of culture having a negative "stigmata" attached to it is actually a reference to the bleeding wounds of the crucifixion left behind on the palms of Jesus Christ. For those who do know the difference, however, it can sure make for some barely suppressed smirks.

STOCKS: A way to employ a middleman in the throwing of your money down the toilet, rather than having to throw it down the toilet yourself.

STOIC:
EXHIBITING NO DISCERNIBLE EMOTION EVEN IN THE FACE OF GREAT SUFFERING. ALSO KNOWN AS BEING MALE.

STONED: A condition capable of making the movie *Seven* seem inexplicably hilarious.

STONEHENGE:

PREHISTORIC GROUPING OF LARGE STANDING STONES IN THE ENGLISH COUNTRYSIDE. BECAUSE IT IS NOT KNOWN HOW AN ANCIENT CULTURE COULD HAVE CONSTRUCTED STONEHENGE, THE MYSTERIOUS SITE ATTRACTS A FAIR PERCENTAGE OF PEOPLE WHO SPEND MOST OF THEIR FREE TIME GOING TO RENAISSANCE FAIRES AND LISTENING TO EITHER YES OR KING CRIMSON.

ST. PATRICK'S DAY:
A DAY ON WHICH MUCH OF THE BEER IS AS GREEN GOING DOWN AS IT IS COMING BACK UP.

STRAIGHT: 1. In a continuous, unbending line. 2. In a continuous, unbending heterosexual relationship.

STREISAND, BARBRA:
WILDLY SUCCESSFUL SINGER AND ACTRESS KNOWN FOR CATERWAULING LIKE THE WHALES SHE IS ALWAYS TRYING TO SAVE.

SUAVE: A word whose connotations of smooth sophistication and debonair charm have been irretrievably tainted by the existence of a line of embarrassingly cut-rate hair-care products.

SUBPRIME: A special lending rate that affords a wealthy banker the same opportunity to achieve total financial ruin as the people he is lending to.

SUBSTITUTE TEACHER: Cannon fodder.

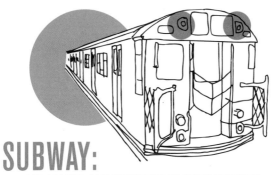

SUBWAY:

1. UNDERGROUND RAILWAY TRANSPORTATION DESIGNED TO QUICKLY AND EFFICIENTLY MOVE COMMUTERS FROM THE SMELL OF FETID URINE TO THE SMELL OF A BASEMENT FULL OF DECAYING BODIES. 2. REGISTERED TRADEMARK OF A CHAIN OF SUBMARINE SANDWICH RESTAURANTS IN WHICH THE EMPLOYEES WEAR CLEAR PLASTIC GLOVES TO REASSURE YOU THAT IF YOU ARE GOING TO GET A DISEASE, IT WILL BE FROM THE FOOD AND NOT FROM THEM.

SUGAR: Another type of addictive white powder that is in its own way as deadly as cocaine and that most people would probably snort if given half a chance.

SUGGESTION: An idea or notion on how to proceed in a given circumstance, submitted for consideration. Not to be attempted in marriage under any circumstances and never to be attempted while driving.

SUGGESTION BOX: A repository for all the ideas your employer ignored when you said them out loud six months ago.

SUMMER: That exquisite time of year when the kids are out of school, the roads jam up, the sweat runs in rivulets from your chest to your navel, and you are forced to sit through the latest movie featuring rapping animated rodents just to get into some air-conditioning.

SUPER BOWL: Thirty-second clips of men running in between highly anticipated commercials.

SUPERMAN: A fictional crime fighter, who somehow became a representative of male potency despite the fact that he goes around in tights, has a cape, and wears his underwear outside his pants.

SUPERMARKET: A retail outlet the size of the Pentagon that gives us a sense of what the Pentagon would be like if it had 109 different kinds of cereal and everyone in the building was each trying to get 96 of them through the ten-items-or-less line.

SURGEON:

A VERY WELL-PAID, KNIFE-WIELDING MANIAC WHO IS ALSO ALLOWED TO WEAR A MASK.

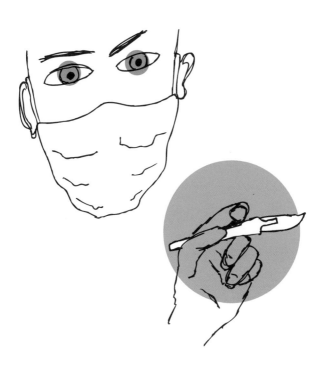

SURGEON, ORAL: Someone whose favorite movie better not be *Marathon Man*.

SURGEON, PLASTIC: A man whom people happily pay to do to their face what most people only experience as punishment for failing to make good on a very large gambling debt.

SUV:

SPORT UTILITY VEHICLE. A TYPE OF AUTOMOTIVE TRANSPORT THAT HAS, FOR SOME UNKNOWN REASON, GOTTEN A BAD RAP JUST BECAUSE, IN TIMES OF WORLD UNREST, DIFFICULT ECONOMIC CIRCUMSTANCES, AND IMPENDING ENVIRONMENTAL DESTRUCTION, ITS FUEL ECONOMY TOPS OUT AT ABOUT 4.2 MILES PER GALLON.

SWEARING: The use of profanity. A vulgar and coarse way of expressing oneself that comes in really handy for everything from bumping one's head to ending a long-term relationship.

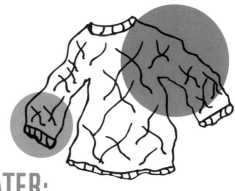

SWEATER:
THE GIFT THAT SAYS, "YES, DEAR, YOU REALLY ARE THAT BORING."

SWIMMING POOL: A useless status symbol that not only costs you a small fortune in upkeep but also requires the services of a swarthy and virile young man to maintain it. Which, let's face it, is pretty much an open invitation for him to regularly ravage your tragically unfulfilled wife while you're at work trying to stay ahead of the payments on the filtration system.

TAJ MAHAL, THE:

SEVENTEENTH-CENTURY MARBLE MONUMENT LOCATED IN INDIA AND KNOWN FOR ITS DOMED, WHITE MAUSOLEUM. AS WITH MANY AN ANCIENT STRUCTURE, IT WAS BUILT BY AN EMPEROR IN HONOR OF ONE OF THE MANY WIVES HE FAVORED. OF COURSE, THESE DAYS, BUILDING A TOWERING EDIFICE TO VENERATE YOUR CHEAP TRAMP CONCUBINE WHORE IS OUT OF THE REACH OF MOST MODERN MARRIED MEN.

TAMPON: A feminine hygiene product that provides a most significant turning point in any relationship. It is that moment when the man is sent to the store to fetch the box of plastic cylinders full of cotton for his girlfriend. Even as he suffers the humiliation of having to publicly purchase such an intimate and even disgusting item, nonetheless he has crossed over into a new level of the devotion and sacrifice he is willing to experience for his counterpart. God, it just makes a person all misty eyed.

TATTOO:

A FORM OF SELF-MUTILATION INTENDED TO ADVERTISE EITHER TOUGHNESS OR SEXUAL PROMISCUITY. WHAT NONE OF THE POSEURS WHO GET NEW INK OR A TRAMP STAMP BY THE MILLIONS REALIZE IS THAT THIS PRACTICE WAS, UNTIL RECENTLY, MOST COMMONLY ASSOCIATED WITH PRISONS, A PLACE WHERE ANY TRAGICALLY HIP CITIFIED PHONY WITH BARBED WIRE ETCHED INTO HIS BICEP WOULD VERY QUICKLY BE SHOWN WHAT TOUGH REALLY MEANS AND WHERE NO ONE GETS A SUNBURST PATTERN ETCHED INTO THEIR LOWER BACK UNLESS SOMETHING REALLY DIRE IS OCCURRING.

TAX: Money we pay to the government with the understanding that they can keep letting everything here go to hell as long as we get to watch them blow stuff up everywhere else.

TEACHER: A person we hire to inform, educate, and mentor our children and who may be the single most important influence outside the family on a child's healthy introduction to society. For this essential, even crucial, contribution to the growth of a society and a nation, teachers are happily paid less than the guy you brought in last week to set up your home theater system.

TEAM PLAYER:
THE MEMBER OF AN ORGANIZATION WHO HAS HIS OR HER NOSE EVER SO FIRMLY WEDGED INTO MANAGEMENT'S BUTT.

TECHNOLOGY: The various applications of scientific, electronic, and digital advancements in the world, without which we would be tragically unable to either annihilate ourselves with the single push of a button or have the results of last night's game delivered directly to our inbox.

TECH SUPPORT:

PEOPLE IN A FOREIGN COUNTRY WHO ARE GETTING PAID ALMOST NOTHING TO BE FRIENDLIER AND MORE HELPFUL THAN PEOPLE IN YOUR OWN COUNTRY COULD EVER HOPE TO BE.

TELEVISION: A smallish box in which live millions of tiny people for you to pity, ridicule, or develop elaborate masturbatory fantasies about.

TEMPLE: Any of various buildings used for gatherings of worship and guilt.

TEXTING: A way of letting people know that actually speaking to them is no longer worth your time.

THANKSGIVING:
A COMPLETE IMPLOSION OF THE FAMILY UNIT, WITH TURKEY.

THERAPIST: Unlike your long-suffering friends, this is the person who will receive some financial remuneration for listening to your incessant, juvenile whining.

THING: All-purpose word relied upon by couples who have been together far too long and therefore cannot be bothered to structure complete commands or sentences. *"Could you get me the thing? I left it over by the thing."*

THINK:

TO REGARD OR APPRAISE IN THE MIND. THIS PROCESS OF REASONING AND DEDUCTION IS UNIQUE TO HUMAN BEINGS, ALTHOUGH IT HAS YET TO BE IN EVIDENCE DURING THE Q&A PORTION OF A BEAUTY PAGEANT.

THUMB: A small, plump digit of the human hand that is next to the index finger. In some animals, the thumb is opposable, meaning it can interact with the four fingers to grip objects. In humans, this had a profound effect on our development, as it allowed us to discover that many everyday items can be used not only as tools but also as very effective implements for clubbing to death those weaker humans who get on our nerves.

TICKET: 1. Written notice of a fine for a parking violation, usually issued owing to our own poor planning, stupidity, or disregard for the law. This is conveniently forgotten in the moment one realizes one has been bagged, and nothing that is actually one's own damn fault has ever been more capable of provoking such righteously indignant fury.

TIME: AN ABSTRACT CONCEPT THAT CAUGHT ON ABOUT SIX THOUSAND YEARS AGO AND RESULTED IN THE CONCEPTS OF BOTH THE DEADLINE AND THE HEART ATTACK, IN THAT ORDER.

TIMES SQUARE:

A GLITTERING, NEON-INFESTED SECTION OF MIDTOWN MANHATTAN FAMOUS FOR ITS THEATERS AND ITS NEW YEAR'S EVE BALL DROP. OF COURSE, THROUGHOUT THE YEAR ONE CAN SEE ALL KINDS OF BALLS DROPPING IN TIMES SQUARE, DEPENDING ON HOW SHORT A SKIRT THE TRANSVESTITE IS WEARING.

TMI: Acronym for *too much information*. Usually employed by repressed people who are too uptight to get a thrill out of graphic descriptions of forbidden lust.

TOILET: A type of chair without which many people would never get any reading done.

TONGUE:
THE PART OF THE HUMAN BODY THAT WAITS ANXIOUSLY BEHIND THE LIPS FOR ITS CHANCE TO ACT MORE FRENCH.

TOUR GUIDE: A nominally paid, frighteningly perky person whose job it is to spew a constant stream of inane information through a poorly wired PA system to distract you from thinking about what a lousy time you are having and/or the fact the air-conditioning on the bus is broken.

TOXIC: 1. The type of poisonous waste that is capable of causing health problems. 2. The type of poisonous human that is capable of boiling a bunny rabbit.

TRAFFIC: Mother's milk to the books-on-tape industry.

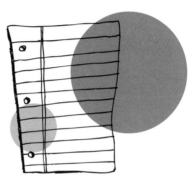

TREE:

DEPENDING ON YOUR WORLDVIEW OR YOUR SPECIES, A TREE IS EITHER AN EXAMPLE OF NATURE'S MAJESTY, A PLACE ON WHICH TO LIFT YOUR LEG WHEN YOU CAN'T FIND A FIRE HYDRANT, OR PAPER WAITING TO HAPPEN.

TROUBLE: A state of distress or difficulty that when you are young involves some infraction against your parents that might get you grounded and when you are older involves some infraction against nature that might put you in the ground.

TRUMP, DONALD:

REAL ESTATE MOGUL WHO CAME TO PROMINENCE DURING THE GREED-BASED CAPITALISM OF THE 1980S; HE HAS HIS OWN REALITY TV SHOW, AND SEVERAL BUILDINGS ARE NAMED AFTER HIM, BUT NO MATTER WHAT HE HAS ACHIEVED, HIS LIFE IS USUALLY REDUCED TO THE PHRASE, "WHAT'S UP WITH THAT HAIR?"

TUNNEL: While in your waking hours, a tunnel is nothing more than an underground passageway. In your dreams, however, it means you are one sick bastard.

TWAIN, MARK:

PEN NAME OF SAMUEL CLEMENS, WILDLY POPULAR NINETEENTH-CENTURY AMERICAN WRITER AND HUMORIST, WHOSE LEGENDARY STATUS DOES NOT EXCUSE THE AMOUNT OF TIMES THE "N" WORD APPEARS IN *THE ADVENTURES OF HUCKLEBERRY FINN.*

TWEAK: To make repeated last-minute minor adjustments to a project. And in so doing, to really cheese off the person who has to print out yet another round of 150 copies for internal distribution just because you belatedly noticed your third obscure infringement on *The Elements of Style* occurring in paragraph five.

TWEE: A quality most commonly found in unsigned indie pop bands, it describes an almost nauseating sweetness, arising from the tragically sincere belief that singing in falsetto about window shopping over a bed of underproduced jangly guitars might actually brighten someone's day.

UFO:

UNIDENTIFIED FLYING OBJECT. SOMETHING MORE PEOPLE
MIGHT BE INCLINED TO BELIEVE IN IF THE PEOPLE WHO
REPORTED THEM WERE NOT ALMOST ALWAYS THE SAME
GAP-TOOTHED TRAILER PARK DENIZENS WHO GET THOSE
OVERSIZED CHECKS FROM THE PUBLISHERS CLEARING
HOUSE.

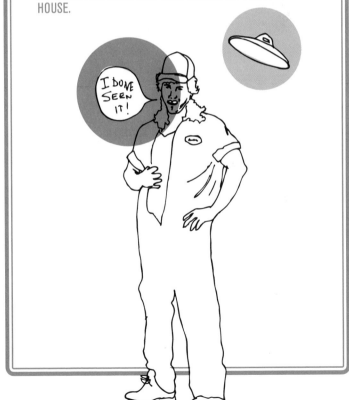

ULTRASOUND: Waves of high-frequency sound used to (a) observe the growth of a fetus and (b) give the prospective father the inexorable, vaguely queasy feeling that there is no way to back out of this damn thing now.

UMBRELLA:

A SEDUCTION TOOL FOR ANYONE WHO CAN ACTUALLY MANAGE TO HOLD A WINDBLOWN PERSONAL CANOPY WHILE PUTTING THEIR ARM AROUND THEIR DATE AT THE SAME TIME AND NOT GETTING SOME PART OF SOMEBODY'S UPPER ANATOMY COMPLETELY SOAKING WET.

UMPIRE: A person trained to communicate his or her feelings by combining elaborate hand gestures with deep, authoritative grunting noises.

UNCLE: A relative whom you keep hearing about from other people: rich, long lost, and dead, as well as having bequeathed his life savings to his favorite niece or nephew. Yet somehow this magical person never appears in your luckless life to croak and make things a little easier.

UNDERCOVER COP:

A REGULAR COP WHO GROWS A BEARD AND LEARNS TO TALK LIKE DENNIS HOPPER.

UNDERWEAR:

A GARMENT WORN BENEATH THE PRIMARY OUTER LAYER OF CLOTHING TO ASSIST US IN BEING LESS AWARE OF OUR GENITALS.

UPLOAD: A process that could take up to eleven hours, depending on your connection speed and how high-resolution you want your pirated copy of *Lethal Weapon IV* to be.

UROLOGIST: Someone who never has to worry about having a pot to piss in.

USER-FRIENDLY: Completely infuriating.

USER NAME: The written characters used for identification when logging on to a Web site; often simply one's name followed by an arbitrary series of numbers assigned by the site itself. Which begs the question: If a monkey hitting random letters on a keyboard for an infinite amount of time would eventually compose the complete works of Shakespeare, how long is it going to take an even mildly intelligent criminal to hack into your online banking account?

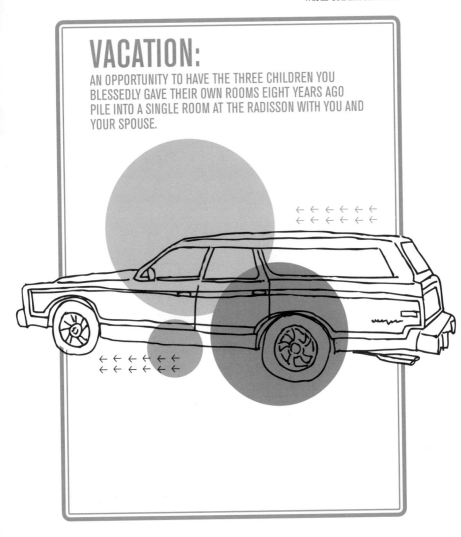

VACATION:

AN OPPORTUNITY TO HAVE THE THREE CHILDREN YOU BLESSEDLY GAVE THEIR OWN ROOMS EIGHT YEARS AGO PILE INTO A SINGLE ROOM AT THE RADISSON WITH YOU AND YOUR SPOUSE.

VALENTINE'S DAY: Celebrated annually on February 14, this is a special day to honor romance. It is calculated to make you feel like a total scumbag if you do not declare your affection for your beloved in some prescribed, materialistic way and to make you feel like a total loser if you do not have a beloved on whom to dump your affection in a prescribed, materialistic way.

VALET: A person who gets more of a workout parking your car than you will ever get driving it.

VAN GOGH, VINCENT:

VISIONARY NINETEENTH-CENTURY POSTIMPRESSIONIST GENIUS WHO BARELY SOLD A SINGLE PAINTING IN HIS LIFETIME. IN FACT, IF HE COULD SEE HIS LIFE'S WORK ON POSTERS, COASTERS, MUGS, AND KEY CHAINS MASS-PRODUCED BY SWEAT SHOPS IN UNDERPRIVILEGED COUNTRIES AND NOT EARNING HIM DOLLAR ONE, HE MIGHT VERY LIKELY CUT OFF HIS EAR AND COMMIT SUICIDE ALL OVER AGAIN.

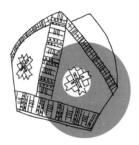

VATICAN, THE:

WHERE THE MAN IN THE FUNNY HAT COMES OUT ON A BALCONY, MAKES A SIGN, AND THEN GOES BACK INSIDE TO HAVE BREAKFAST ON A PLATE THAT COSTS MORE THAN YOUR HOUSE.

VEGAN: People whose grain-, nut-, and soy-based diet excludes all meat, fish, and dairy products. While one may think this a bland and wimpy way to live, make no mistake: These people produce monstrous, formidable, bottom burps that rival the noxious wind produced by any meat eater on the planet.

VEGETARIAN: A vegan who didn't have the balls to give up cheese.

VETERINARIAN: A physician who has the luxury of working with patients who cannot ask him or her any annoying questions while being probed by some form of tubing.

VIAGRA:

A SURE SIGN THAT MODERN SCIENCE HAS ITS PRIORITIES STRAIGHT. CANCER, LEUKEMIA, AND WORLD HUNGER CAN WAIT. SOMEBODY NEEDS TO GET GOING ON A FOUR-HOUR ERECTION.

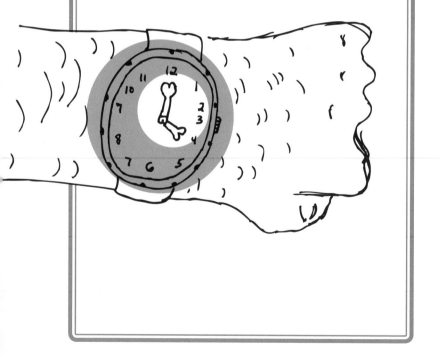

VICE PRESIDENT: An executive position below the rank of president. In the corporate world, vice presidents are responsible for a variety of duties, often with more daily responsibility even than the CEO to whom they report, whereas in the political arena, the vice president's job is simply to wait around on the off chance that the other guy dies.

VIRTUAL: An online universe for people who lied to their parents *and* the child psychologist all those years ago when they swore they no longer had the compulsion to play with imaginary friends.

VOICE MAIL: WHERE YOU SEND THE DOZENS OF PEOPLE YOU CAN NO LONGER TOLERATE AND WHERE YOU YOURSELF ARE SENT MORE TIMES THAN YOU KNOW.

VOLLEYBALL: A once innocuous and even goofy sport that has in recent years been completely legitimized by a bunch of hot chicks in spandex bikinis.

VOTING:

THE AGONIZING CHOICE MADE AT EACH ELECTION CYCLE BETWEEN SOMEONE WHO WAS ABLE TO SPEND $54 MILLION ON CAMPAIGN ADVERTISING AND SOMEONE ELSE WHO WAS ONLY ABLE TO AFFORD $53.5 MILLION.

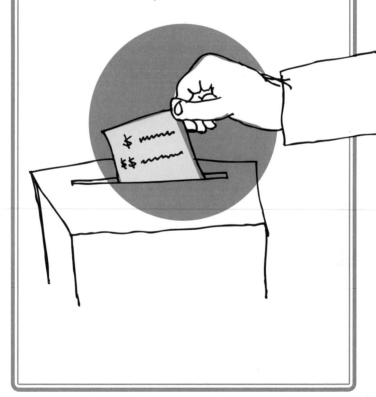

WAISTLINE:

THE PART OF THE HUMAN BODY THAT WE GET THE MOST OBSESSIVE ABOUT KEEPING TRIM, IF ONLY TO REMAIN DESIRABLE ENOUGH SO ACTIVITY OCCURRING BELOW IT WILL STILL BE A VIABLE OPTION.

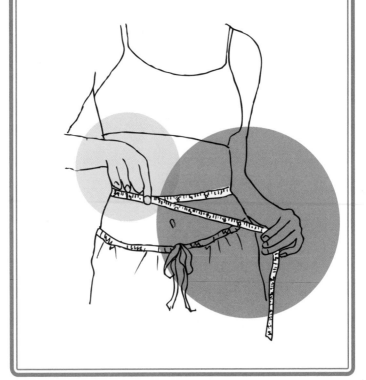

WAITER:
↓ ↓

→ Actor.

WAITING ROOM:

A PLACE TO PASS THE TIME BY TAKING FURTIVE GLANCES AT THE OTHER MORIBUND UNFORTUNATES AROUND YOU WHILE WONDERING WHICH PART OF THEIR BODY WILL SOON BE PROBED BY A MEDICAL PROFESSIONAL.

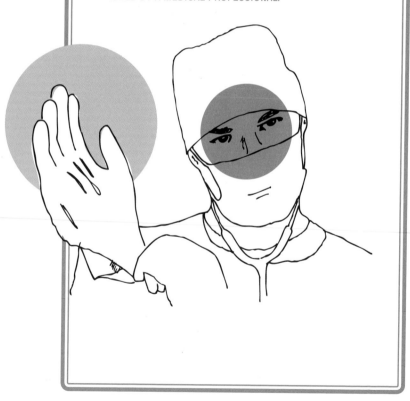

WAITRESS:

↓ ↓

→ Actress.

WALK: An unpleasant option that one is forced to take to get from one's front door to one's car.

WALL STREET JOURNAL, THE: Birdcage liner with a touch of class.

WAR: A state of antagonism and conflict between states, nations, or even individuals, such as the kind of hostilities engaged in during a personal rivalry or divorce. In the case of the latter, a homicidal former spouse combined with the right sadistic lawyer may drain more blood from the opposition than has ever been seen on a battlefield.

WASHINGTON, GEORGE:

FIRST PRESIDENT OF THE UNITED STATES AND PIONEER OF THE FIERCELY EROTIC POWDERED-WIG LOOK THAT WOULD DOMINATE THE PRESIDENCY RIGHT THROUGH TO THAT STUD JAMES MADISON.

WASHINGTON MONUMENT:

DESCRIBED IN THE GUIDEBOOKS AS THE WORLD'S TALLEST OBELISK, WHEN IT IS PERFECTLY CLEAR TO ANYONE THAT IT IS A PHALLIC SYMBOL STRAIGHT OUT OF A FREUDIAN FEVER DREAM. TRYING TO LIVE UP TO THIS IMPOSSIBLE MALE IDEAL IS PART OF WHAT GETS THE UNITED STATES INTO SO MUCH TROUBLE.

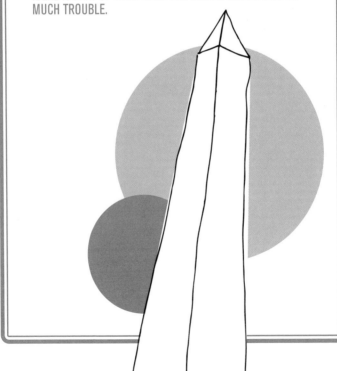

WATER: The substance without which all human, plant, and animal life would cease to exist, and which, in fact, may one day run out, thus plunging the world into a *Road Warrior*–type nightmare in which rogue bands of psychotics are willing to kill just for a drop of it. But that's a long way off, so go ahead and take that fifteen-minute shower.

WAXING: Hair removal for masochists.

WEATHER: A natural phenomenon created by God to give boring people something to talk about.

WEATHERMAN:
A JOB CREATED BY TELEVISION TO GIVE BORING PEOPLE SOMETHING TO TALK ABOUT ON CAMERA.

WEB SITE: An Internet destination wherein you can find out everything you ever wanted to know about a subject you previously had no interest in.

WEDDING: A glorious occasion in which family, friends, and loved ones come from miles around for the pleasure of staying mum about the terrible mistake you are making.

WELL ENDOWED: A condition that can be faked on a woman but only lied about by a man.

WELLES, ORSON: The guy who directed that tedious movie they made you watch in college.

WELLS, H.G.: Late-nineteenth and early-twentieth-century science fiction writer whose novels posited the possibility of invisibility, time travel, and an invasion of earth by hostile space aliens. While none of these eventualities have ever come about, it hasn't stopped Hollywood from subjecting us to repackaged versions of this claptrap every couple of years for the rest of our natural lives.

WHITE: A condition thrust upon a certain percentage of the population by birth, requiring them to enjoy mayonnaise, boxed wine, and the soundtrack to *The Big Chill*.

WHY:

A QUESTION THAT A FOUR-YEAR-OLD CAN ASK IN SUCH STAGGERING NUMBERS THAT EVENTUALLY YOU REALIZE TIME HAS NO MEANING AND YOU ARE TRAPPED IN AN ENDLESS LOOP OF SYLLOGISTIC LOGIC THAT SPINS BACK ON ITSELF UNTIL THE TOP OF YOUR HEAD BLOWS UP LIKE THAT GUY IN *SCANNERS*.

WIFE: A woman who, one way or another, is going to end up wearing the pants.

WI-FI: A service provided by many coffeehouses to give their good-for-nothing patrons yet another reason to spend all day sitting there without buying anything.

WII: A VIDEO GAME CONSOLE THAT PROVIDES GALLING NEW WAYS TO PRETEND YOU ARE GETTING EXERCISE.

WIKIPEDIA: An online adventure in higher learning, where the entry for the Second World War is likely to be several paragraphs shorter than the one on *The Brady Bunch*.

WILDE, OSCAR: Nineteenth-century humorist, author, and dandy who was sent to prison for acts of indecency with other men. Thankfully, we now live in a world where flamboyant pioneers like Wilde can be readily accepted by society at large—as long as they are confined to television programs, where they are inevitably cast as the wacky but sensitive neighbor of the female lead.

WILL: Your last chance to let your children know where they rank in descending order of importance.

WINDOWS:

THE OPERATING SYSTEM AND INTERFACES MADE BY MICROSOFT CORPORATION. SO NAMED BECAUSE OF WHAT THEY MAKE YOU WANT TO JUMP OUT OF WHEN USING THEM.

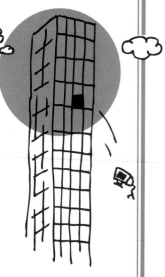

WINE: A way to get drunk that does not make you belch.

WINTER: A challenge issued by nature itself to see how sexy someone can look while dressed in layers.

WOMAN: A female adult, or wench if you want to get a knee in the groin.

WORKAHOLIC: Someone who uses their job to get some well-deserved time away from loved ones.

WORKPLACE: A location at which dealing with incompetents, morons, and even a certain amount of abuse is more than offset by the free computer.

WRESTLING:
BOXING WITH HAIR.

WRIGHT BROTHERS, THE:

ORVILLE AND WILBUR, WHO FAMOUSLY MADE THE FIRST CONTROLLED AIRPLANE FLIGHT IN 1903. THIS WAS IMMEDIATELY FOLLOWED BY THE FIRST REMINDER THAT THE CONTENTS OF THE OVERHEAD BINS MAY HAVE SHIFTED.

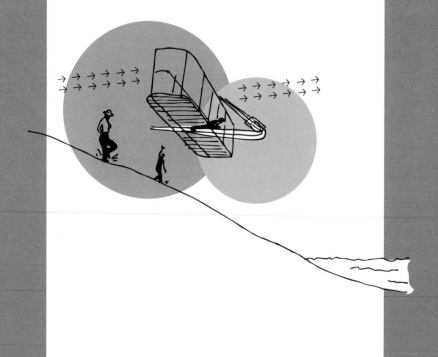

WRITER: A person who is certain they are capable of producing *War and Peace* and cannot understand why they are getting paid ten bucks a pop to crank out articles on decoupage for some advertiser-supported arts and crafts blog.

WRONG: What nobody likes to admit they are until after the dynamite make-up sex.

WYSIWYG: What You See Is What You Get. A computing term used to indicate that you don't need to spend half a day typing in a buttload of HTML code just to get your document to look like what it's supposed to. Take that, you sanctimonious Mac users.

XENOPHOBIA: An irrational fear or distrust of strangers or foreigners. Like we needed a nice word for *narrow-minded, racist pud-whack*.

X-RAY: Electromagnetic radiation used to take photographic impressions of the human body. A process made no more comforting by the fact that the technician asks you to hold your breath after handing you a twenty-five-pound lead-based shield that could probably deflect bullets but will likely do nothing to prevent your impending sterility.

XYLOPHONE:
A SLEEPING PILL IN PERCUSSION FORM.

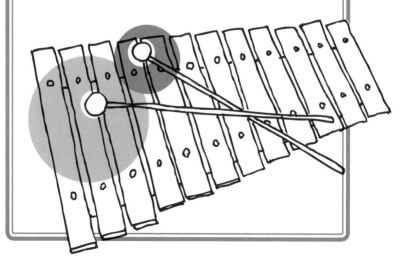

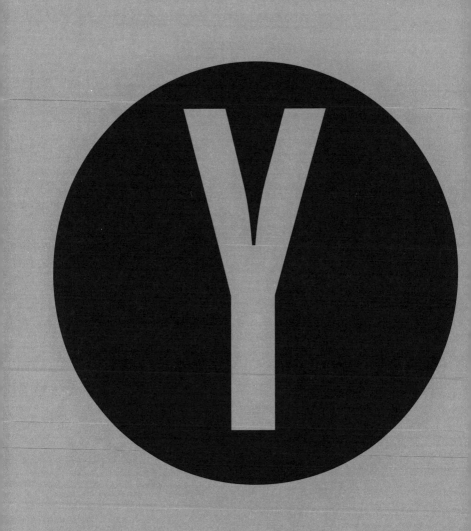

YAHOO!: The other Internet search engine, whose awkwardness as a verb prevented it from entering the nomenclature like Google did. (No getting around it, *I Yahooed myself last weekend* just doesn't have quite the same ring.)

YARD SALE:

THE LAST RESORT FOR THE DESPERATE SHOPPER, WHO WILL DIE WITHOUT A CERAMIC POODLE BEDSIDE LAMP, A NAPKIN HOLDER FROM THE CUMBERLAND GAP HISTORICAL PARK, OR ONE OF THE 5,347,201 REMAINING PAPERBACK COPIES OF *THE PELICAN BRIEF*.

YEAR: Three hundred and sixty-five days. Or, as it is known in Montana, half an hour.

YELLOW:

THE COLOR A TRAFFIC LIGHT TURNS WHEN IT IS INDICATING THAT YOU SHOULD FLOOR IT.

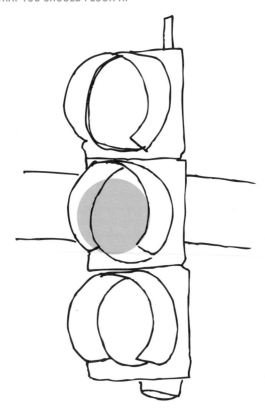

YES: A hastily uttered word that has caused many an unwanted job, pregnancy, and, perhaps worst of all, commitment to helping your friends move.

YESTERDAY: What anything that wasn't invented a week ago is to a teenager.

YOGA:
A SPIRITUAL DISCIPLINE AIMED AT GUIDING A PERSON TOWARD A DEEPER SENSE OF HIS OR HER OWN HUMANITY, WHOSE MOST WELL KNOWN POSITION IS THE DOWNWARD-FACING DOG.

YOGURT: Milk that has been allowed to curdle through interaction with bacteria, available in handy single-serving sizes for the kids.

YOU: The person it's usually all about, let's face it.

YOUNG: Not yet able to grasp how much pop music sucks.

YOUTUBE: An Internet outlet for a bunch of talent-free, antisocial pariahs that makes the misfit-generated programming on your local public-access television station look like *Masterpiece Theatre*.

ZAFTIG: Full-figured; a pleasingly plump state that was considered quite attractive for generations, until the fashion and diet industries made everyone aspire to look like the people in UNICEF commercials.

ZAMBONI:

A VEHICLE THAT SMOOTHES THE SURFACE OF HOCKEY RINKS. AND IF IT SUCKS UP ALL THE BLOOD IN THE PROCESS, SO MUCH THE BETTER.

ZANY: Trying to be funny by pinwheeling one's arms and making high-pitched, guttural Jerry Lewis noises. Never works.

ZEALOUS: Fervently committed to being so fervently committed that nobody wants to talk to you anymore.

ZEBRA:

AN ANIMAL WITH THE UNFORTUNATE BURDEN OF A COAT THAT MAKES IT LOOK FAT.

The Official Dictionary of Sarcasm

ZEITGEIST:

THE TENOR AND MOOD OF AN AGE. THIS IS A WORD MOST
COMMONLY USED BY WINE-AND-CHEESE INTELLECTUALS AT
ART GALLERY OPENINGS, WHO ARE, IN REALITY, SO OUT OF
TOUCH WITH THE ZEITGEIST THAT THEY THINK A PAINTING
OF A RED BLOTCH ON A CANVAS MADE OF NAUGAHYDE
ACTUALLY SAYS SOMETHING ABOUT LIFE AS WE KNOW IT.

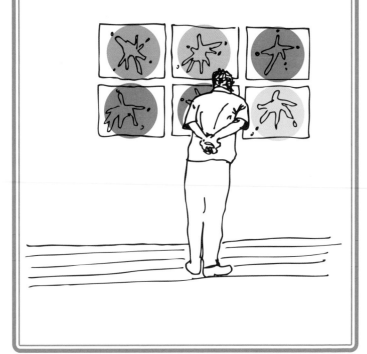

ZEST: A feeling of effervescent exuberance and engagement in the simple act of living. And only a notch or two away from taking that step into cross-dressing.

ZIGZAG: Movement in an angular pattern punctuated by sharp twists and turns. Also a brand of rolling paper, whose papers when filled with the substance they are most commonly associated with create a similar sensation.

ZILLION: A nonspecific, very high number. More than a million, but slightly less than, say, all the people who hate brussels sprouts.

ZIPPER:

WHAT HAPPENED WHEN SOMEBODY SAID, "HEY, LET'S GET TWO ROWS OF METAL TEETH AND PUT THEM RIGHT NEXT TO OUR REPRODUCTIVE ORGANS!"

ZIRCONIA, CUBIC: A diamond that is decidedly *not* forever.

ZIT: A pustule that forms most prevalently during adolescence, so that as you become more aware of your changing body, the world becomes more aware of your appalling face.

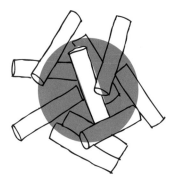

ZITI: TUBE-SHAPED PASTA THAT GETS ITS NAME FROM THE PLURAL FORM OF THE ITALIAN WORD FOR BRIDEGROOM. JEEZ, WHY DIDN'T THEY JUST CALL IT "BAKED DOINKER"?

ZODIAC: An imaginary system of divination that allows dimwits to blame their lackluster dating history, unemployability, and poor driving skills on the position Uranus was in at the moment they breached the womb.

ZOMBIE: A walking corpse. One can become a zombie either by having one's brains sucked out by another zombie or by getting a job.

ZOO: Dreary, panting, captive animals being pointed at by ignoramuses all day, not even granted the privacy any of us would want when hurling our own feces. Truly, one of the most uplifting family outings one could possibly imagine.

ZYGOTE: The approximate developmental stage of the little twerp to whom they just gave your old job.

ABOUT THE AUTHOR

Now, this is the part of the book where they tell you what other meaningless drivel the author has written (in this case, *The North Pole Employee Handbook, Violation! The Ultimate Ticket Book,* and *Christmas Letters Gone Wild,* as if you care). Then it's on to whether the author is married and, if so, what the names of his or her spouse and children are (I suppose it wouldn't be good form to say that they were around at one time but have long since been driven away by the author's megalomania and manic-depressive tendencies). Oh, and then it's on to where the author lives, at which point it is always a good idea to imply that the author divides his or her time between two or more cities. It just seems much more writerly and gives one the impression that a reclusive, embittered fool is actually a cosmopolitan jet-setter.

There, satisfied?

STERLING, the Sterling logo, STERLING INNOVATION, and the Sterling
Innovation logo are registered trademarks of Sterling Publishing Co., Inc.

Library of Congress Cataloging-in-Publication Data Available

20 19 18 17

Published by Sterling Publishing Co., Inc.
387 Park Avenue South, New York, NY 10016
© 2010 by Sterling Publishing Co., Inc.
Distributed in Canada by Sterling Publishing
c/o Canadian Manda Group, 165 Dufferin Street
Toronto, Ontario, Canada M6K 3H6
Distributed in the United Kingdom by GMC Distribution Services
Castle Place, 166 High Street, Lewes, East Sussex, England BN7 1XU
Distributed in Australia by Capricorn Link (Australia) Pty. Ltd.
P.O. Box 704, Windsor, NSW 2756, Australia

Cover and interior design by: Ohioboy Art & Design / www.ohioboy.com
All illustrations by Andy Taray, Christy Taray, and Christian Woltman for
Ohioboy Art & Design.

Printed in China
All rights reserved

Sterling ISBN 978-1-4027-6952-8

For information about custom editions, special sales, premium and
corporate purchases, please contact Sterling Special Sales
Department at 800-805-5489 or specialsales@sterlingpublishing.com.